Science education for
a pluralist society

DEVELOPING SCIENCE AND TECHNOLOGY EDUCATION

Series Editor: Brian Woolnough,
Department of Educational Studies, University of Oxford

Current titles:

John Eggleston: *Teaching Design and Technology*
David Layton: *Technology's Challenge to Science Education*
Keith Postlethwaite: *Differentiated Science Teaching*
Michael J. Reiss: *Science Education for a Pluralist Society*
Jon Scaife and Jerry Wellington: *Information Technology in Science and Technology Education*
Joan Solomon: *Teaching Science, Technology and Society*
Clive Sutton: *Words, Science and Learning*

Titles in preparation include:

Richard Gott and Sandra Duggan: *Investigative Work in Science*
Michael Poole: *Beliefs and Values in Science Education*
Brian Woolnough: *Effective Science Teaching*

Science education for a pluralist society

MICHAEL J. REISS

Open University Press
Buckingham · Philadelphia

Open University Press   *507.12
Celtic Court
22 Ballmoor
Buckingham
MK18 1XW

and

1900 Frost Road, Suite 101
Bristol, PA 19007, USA

First Published 1993

A catalogue record of this book is available from the British Library

0 335 15760 2 (pb)   0 335 15761 0 (hb)

Library of Congress Cataloging-in-Publication Data

Reiss, Michael J. (Michael Jonathan), 1958–
    Science education for a pluralist society / Michael J. Reiss.
        p.   cm. — (Developing science and technology education)
    Includes bibliographical references and index.
    ISBN 0–335–15761–0.   ISBN 0–335–15760–2 (pbk.)
    1. Science–Study and teaching.   2. Science – Study and teaching –
Social aspects.   3. Pluralism (Social sciences).   I. title.
II. Series.
Q181.R43   1993
507′.12 – dc20   92–47138
CIP

Typeset by Type Study, Scarborough
Printed in Great Britain by St Edmundsbury Press,
Bury St Edmunds, Suffolk

To Tony Adams, Alan Bishop and Anna King

Contents

Series editor's preface

It may seem surprising that after three decades of curriculum innovation, and with the increasing provision of a centralized National Curriculum, that it is felt necessary to produce a series of books which encourages teachers and curriculum developers to continue to rethink how science and technology should be taught in schools. But teaching can never be merely the 'delivery' of someone else's 'given' curriculum. It is essentially a personal and professional business in which lively, thinking, enthusiastic teachers continue to analyse their own activities and mediate the curriculum framework to their students. If teachers ever cease to be critical of what they are doing, then their teaching, and their students' learning, will become sterile.

There are still important questions which need to be addressed, questions which remain fundamental but the answers to which may vary according to the social conditions and educational priorities at a particular time.

What is the justification for teaching science and technology in our schools? For educational or vocational reasons? Providing science and technology for all, for future educated citizens, or to provide adequately prepared and motivated students to fulfil the industrial needs of the country? Will the same type of curriculum satisfactorily meet both needs or do we need a differentiated curriculum? In the past it has too readily been assumed that one type of science will meet all needs.

What should be the nature of science and technology in schools? It will need to develop both the methods and the content of the subject, the way a scientist or engineer works and the appropriate knowledge and understanding, but what is the relationship between the two? How does the student's explicit knowledge relate to investigational skill, how important is the student's tacit knowledge? In the past the holistic nature of scientific activity and the importance of affective factors such as commitment and enjoyment have been seriously undervalued in relation to the student's success.

And, of particular concern to this series, what is the relationship between science and technology? In some countries the scientific nature of technology and the technological aspects of science make the subjects a natural continuum. In others the curriculum structures have separated the two, leaving the teachers to develop appropriate links. Underlying this series is the belief that science and technology have an important interdependence and thus many of the books will be appropriate to teachers of both science and technology.

Many of us grew up believing that science was an activity done by men, white Anglo-saxon men, probably wearing glasses and a white lab coat. Certainly this caricature is held by the vast majority of young people in schools. I suspect that many still believe that all the really important scientific theories and discoveries were made in western culture, in England, Europe or possibly the USA. Michael Reiss has done a great service in exploding such myths by bringing together such a comprehensive collection of examples of science and scientific thinking by non-Western, non-male scientists. In this scholarly yet practical book the sheer weight of examples carries conviction and is unlikely to leave the most hardened WASP un-moved. By grouping so many examples within the areas of the attainment targets of the Science in the English and Welsh National Curriculum (or within the areas of Biology, Chemistry and Physics for those not using this curriculum framework!) teach-ers will be able readily to incorporate examples from different cultural backgrounds into their daily teaching programmes.

But this book is more than a collection of examples of science and scientists emanating from a wide range of cultures. It proposes and discusses a philosophy for science teaching, a teaching approach and methodology which could funda-mentally transform the perception that pupils gain of science, and of different cultural traditions. For this book is about more than science teaching, it is about appreciating and valuing individuals from quite different cultures and that must be important in our pluralist society.

Brian E. Woolnough

Preface and acknowledgements

When I first became interested in multicultural and anti-racist science education, I went, as any good science educator in the UK would, to the Association for Science Education's *Science Teachers' Handbook*. There I found only a section called 'Science education and ethnic minorities' and that in a chapter titled 'Special problems' (Nellist and Nicholl, 1986). Things have moved on since then. Recent years have seen an increasing acknowledgement that the science taught in schools is nearly always narrow in its approach and one-sided in its implicit assumptions. During the 1980s it was realized that most school science was essentially 'male' and 'Western' in focus, teaching style, content and assessment. By now it is increasingly being understood that the model of science held, the way science is taught and the specific content matter learned are all too often restricted in outlook.

The consequences of a narrow, male, Western view of school science are far reaching and of two main sorts. First, many pupils quite correctly feel alienated from school science and drop it once they can. Secondly, the minority of pupils and students who go on to study science once they have the choice whether to or not, continue to learn an impoverished form of science.

A valid science education for a pluralist society will encourage and permit greater equality of standing between science as carried out and perceived by different cultural, ethnic, gender, class and religious groups. It can be contrasted with the present prevalent model of science education which leads to non-Western, non-male, non-atheistic science simply being ignored. It is my hope that this book will help contribute to such a pluralist society. It is unfortunate that this book, as is the case for all the books in Open University Press's *Developing Science and Technology Education* series, has on its front cover a version of da Vinci's celebrated renaissance male. Whether it is significant that he has been emasculated, I will leave the reader to judge.

The author gratefully acknowledges permission to reproduce the following material: **Figure 2.1**, reproduced by permission of Royal Mail and Giant Limited; **Figure 2.2**, Caroline Allen; **Figure 2.3**, Chris Madden; **Figure 2.4**, copyright British Museum; **Figure 3.1**, Jacky Fleming; Penguin Books; **Figure 3.2**, R. Needham and P. Hill (1987) *Children's Learning in Science Project: Teaching Strategies for Developing Understanding in Science*, Centre for Studies in Science and Mathematics Education, The University, Leeds, p.7; **Figure 4.1**, Gerald; The Windmill School, Cambridgeshire; **Figure 4.2**, Hobsons Publishing plc; **Figure 4.4**, Tarik Chawdry; **Figure 4.5**, Peter and Susan Norman; Jacky Chapman; **Figure, 5.1**, Clive Offley; *New Internationalist*; **Figure 5.2**, Taken from B. Knapp (1986) *Systematic Geography*, Allen & Unwin, p. 342; **Figure 5.3**, Associated Press; **Figure 6.1**, reprinted by permission of the publishers from *The Healing Hand: Man and Wound in the Ancient World* by Guido Majno, Cambridge, Mass.: Harvard University Press, copyright © 1975 by the President and Fellows of

Harvard College; **Figure 6.2**, copyright British Museum; **Figure 6.3**, G. A. Perry and M. J. D. Hirons (1970) *Progressive Biology: Book 3*, Blandford Press, London, p. 12; **Figure 6.4**, A. Agarwal and S. Narain (1991) Global warming in an unequal world, *New Internationalist*, April, p. 11, Centre for Science and Development, New Delhi; **Figure 7.1**, Peter Schmidt; **Figure 7.2**, Griffith Institute, Ashmolean Museum, Oxford; **Figure 7.3**, Imperial War Museum; **Figure 7.4**, Marie Curie Cancer Care; **Figure 7.5**, Trustees of the Science Museum; **Figure 8.1a**, *Activate 1* (Autumn term 1992, p. 2), the energy magazine for schools published by the UK Atomic Energy Authority; **Figure 8.1b**, *Science 19* (Association for Science Education, p. 14); **Figure 8.2**, J. Walker (1985) *Roundabout: The Physics of Rotation in the Everyday World. Readings from 'The Amateur Scientist' in SCIENTIFIC AMERICAN*, W. H. Freeman, New York, p. 52; **Figure 8.4**, State Samarqand Museum of History, Architecture and Arts.

I am especially grateful to all of the following who either commented on portions of the manuscript or helped me by giving me their time in valuable discussions or correspondence: Madeleine Arnot, Alan Bishop, John Siraj-Blatchford, Andrew Davies, Mohinder Galowalia, Tony Hewish, Liz Jackson, Edgar Jenkins, Brenda Jennison, Nick Jordan, Anna King, Terry McLaughlin, Peter Mitchell, Masakata Ogawa, Alan Peacock, Michael Poole, Nicholas Postgate, John Raffan, Zulfikar Sayeed, Dafila Scott, Steve Thorp, Sheila Turner, Tony Turner and Paul Warwick. Particular thanks are due to Brian Woolnough, who read through the entire manuscript, and to John Skelton for his patience and efficiency.

CHAPTER 1

What this book is about

In 1904 Edith Patch was appointed as an entomologist at the University of Maine. One agricultural writer pronounced it a mistake because 'a woman could not climb a tree'; another noted that she would 'have a hard time catching grasshoppers'. By the time she died, Edith Patch had published fifteen books and almost one hundred academic papers and had been a President of the Entomological Association of America.

(Ogilvie, 1986: 144)

There are two main justifications for what can be termed 'pluralistic science education'. First, that it is a more just education; secondly, that it is better science education. In this book I will try to defend each of these assertions. In this chapter I will clarify my use of some specialist terms and provide outlines of later chapters. I will start by describing what are meant by 'multicultural science education', 'anti-racist science education' and 'girl-friendly, feminine and feminist science education' and relate these to 'pluralistic science education'.

Multicultural science education

Multicultural science education starts from the fundamental premise that the science taught in most schools is too narrow in its focus (Williams, 1983; Science for a Multicultural Society Group, 1985; Turner and Turner, 1989a; Secondary Science Curriculum Review, n.d.). Specifically:

1 School science is often divorced from its historical and international context.
2 When science is put in an historical context in schools, that context is often biased, with the work of white scientists being overemphasized.
3 Despite recent curricular initiatives, school science is still often portrayed in such a way that traditional activities such as agriculture, cooking, the making of clothes and the design of homes are not seen to fall within the definition of science.

(Reiss, 1993)

Multicultural science emphasizes the contributions made by *all* scientists. This is an important part of good science teaching. Too many pupils have no idea of the extent and significance of the contributions made to science by non-Western cultures. For example, the following were all known about, invented or used in China hundreds of years before they were 'discovered' in the West:

the compass, magnetic remanence and induction, the iron plough, the 'modern' horse harness, the multi-tube seed drill, sunspots, quantitative cartography, solar wind, 'Mercator' map-projection, cast iron, the crank handle, deep drilling for natural gas, the suspension bridge, underwater salvage operations, paper, the wheelbarrow, sliding callipers, the fishing reel, the stirrup, porcelain, biological pest control, the umbrella, matches, chess, brandy, whisky, the mechanical clock, printing, paper money, the spinning-wheel, endocrinology, diabetes, immunology, medicinal use of thyroxine, the decimal system, zero, negative numbers, Pascal's [*sic*] triangle, Newton's [*sic*] First Law, the seismograph, phosphorescent paint, the kite, the parachute, masts, hermetically sealed laboratories, chemical warfare, the crossbow, gunpowder and the rocket.

(Temple, 1991)

Although important, considerable care needs to be taken in incorporating examples of multicultural science into one's teaching. First, any appearance of tokenism may be self-defeating. Secondly, appearing to 'push' a particular line may be counterproductive. Thirdly, many pupils are not especially interested in the history of science. Fourthly, few science teachers are likely to have a background in the history of science. Finally, there is a different sort of danger about multicultural teaching. It can become patronising and voyeuristic (Gill *et al.*, 1987). Multicultural science education on its own is not enough. It needs to be accompanied by anti-racist science education.

Anti-racist science education

At a whole-school level, considerable agreement exists as to what constitutes anti-racist education. Fundamentally, anti-racist education seeks actively to challenge educational inequalities based on race, ethnicity, culture or religion (though some would object to the inclusion of the word 'race', on the grounds that even its use here falsely lends credence to racist ideas, behaviours, attitudes and practice). Anti-racist education aims to counteract and combat attitudes and behaviours which lead to prejudice, discrimination and injustice (Brandt, 1986; Troyna, 1987; McLean and Young, 1988; Grinter, 1989; Maitland, 1989; National Union of Teachers, 1989; Bishop, 1990).

Anti-racist science education tries to help achieve these aims through science teaching (Lindsay, 1985; Gill and Levidow, 1987; Reiss, 1990; Brophy, 1991). Successful anti-racist science education enables people better to understand what science is. It helps people challenge things that can all too often go unquestioned. For example, an anti-racist approach to the topic of human populations might challenge the widely held view that overpopulation is the fault of people in Third World/developing/non-industrialized countries. Few pupils appreciate the many factors which affect average family size, or realize that most First World countries support a greater density of people than do most Third World countries.

Often an effective way of ensuring an anti-racist perspective on the teaching of a particular science topic is to ask *why* certain things are so, or *what* causes certain things:

- Why do famines happen?
- Why has malaria been eradicated from most of Europe but from little of Africa?
- What causes soil erosion?

Girl-friendly, feminine and feminist science education

Much of school science is still seen by many pupils as being an appropriate activity for boys, but an inappropriate activity for most girls. Bentley and Watts (1986) argue that there are three types of answer to the question: 'What should science education for girls be like?'. The first they call 'girl-friendly science'. Here, for instance, teachers expand their teaching by including activities such as bread-baking and crystal growing to encourage girls to come to lunch-time girls-only science clubs. In the experience of teachers working within the Girls into Science and Technology (GIST) project, this approach encouraged girls to join the clubs. Once girls' confidence had been gained, activities such as building electronics circuits were included (Smail, 1984). As Bentley and Watts point out, the essence of this approach is to induce girls into a science that is essentially unchanged.

The second approach discussed by Bentley and Watts (1986) they call 'feminine science'. Here the emphasis is on (i) the consideration of social, ethical and moral questions; (ii) co-operation and respect for different forms of knowledge, including the subjective. This leads to:

> a vision of pupils being encouraged into a science education which makes much of feelings and engagement with issues, and with co-operation in working groups. In such groups, ideals would be welcomed because people have the courage and commitment to put them forward, and would not be evaluated and then dismissed by other individuals almost as a matter of course.
>
> (Bentley and Watts, 1986: 125)

The final approach described by Bentley and Watts is 'feminist science'. This challenges the common assumption as to what science is (discussed in more detail in Chapter 2). Bentley and Watts argue, first, that feminist science emphasizes a philosophy of wisdom rather than a philosophy of knowledge as the driving force that should be behind science; and secondly, that feminist science creates an investigative paradigm which encourages subjectivity and in which feelings, values and intuitions are an essential part.

I can imagine two sorts of reactions among readers unfamiliar with the arguments in favour of feminist science being learned by all pupils, not just girls. Some readers may feel that the shutters have fallen from their eyes; that this is what they have been waiting for. Perhaps, though, a common reaction will be to be suspicious at an approach which appears to advocate subjectivity at the expense of objectivity. I will try to show in Chapter 2 that the acknowledgement that science is not as universal as has often been supposed does not mean that all claims to objectivity must be abandoned.

Pluralistic science education

Pluralistic science education incorporates all that is best in the above three categories – multicultural science education, anti-racist science education and feminist science education – and more. A pluralist society would be one in which there was equality of standing between all the different groups of people making up that society. In addition to addressing issues to do with gender and ethnicity, pluralistic science education strives for equality (not just of opportunity, but of outcome) for peoples of different class, religion and disability. Although some work is now being done on the subject of science education for pupils with disabilities (discussed in Chapter 4), disappointingly little has yet been published in relation to religion and class.

Alternative terms for 'pluralistic science education' include 'science education for all' (in the literal, not the pejorative, sense of the phrase) and 'equal opportunities science education'.

Other specialist terms and language issues

The following should be noted:

- 'Black' is taken to mean 'non-white'.
- 5–16-year-olds receiving school education are referred to as 'pupils'. 'Students' is used to refer to 16–19-year-olds receiving school education and to those receiving Further or Higher Education.
- Usually 'she' and 'her' refer to women or girls. Occasionally, they are used inclusively to refer to someone of either gender.
- I have used the Christian system for dating years, though BCE (Before the Common Era) is used in preference to BC (Before Christ) and, when it is needed, CE (Common Era) is used in preference to AD (Anno Domini).
- Married women are named by the surnames they used themselves.
- No attempt has been made to indicate how names should be pronounced.
- The traditional Western forms of Semitic names have mostly been used.
- The terms 'Third World', 'developing countries', 'non-industrialized countries' and 'non-Western countries' are used interchangeably for want of a really suitable term.

Outline of chapters

Chapter 2, 'What is science?', outlines the contemporary debate about the nature of science and begins to relate it to science teaching in schools. The contributions of historians of science, philosophers of science, sociologists of science and science educationalists are examined, as is the relationship between science and technology and between science and religion.

Chapter 3, 'Science curricula for a pluralist society' criticizes the adoption of a Western, male view of science in school syllabuses and textbooks. It looks at the aims of school science and also attempts to answer the important question: 'Why aren't there more black/women scientists?'

Chapter 4, 'A science department for all', draws

together examples of good practice and tries to suggest what a school science department that was appropriate for all learners might be like in its staffing, organization, appearance and teaching methods.

Chapter 5, 'Teaching controversial issues in science' looks at the strengths and weaknesses of the various approaches that are used for teaching controversial issues in school science. It includes suggestions for the teaching of particular science topics.

Chapters 6, 7 and 8 contain a large number of examples intended to help a teacher who wishes to adopt the approach to science education advocated in this book. Most of the examples are therefore of contributions to science made by non-Westerners and/or women. The question as to what constitutes science is discussed in Chapter 2, but in these chapters I have accepted a conventional school-type understanding of the domain of science. I have excluded contributions to mathematics (see Bishop, 1988; Ascher, 1991; Harris, 1991; Shan and Bailey, 1991; Joseph, 1992) and to a number of scientific disciplines that may be said to sit at the edge of mainstream science – computing, engineering, anthropology and psychology. I have also excluded examples that most readers would consider to fall more appropriately within the disciplines of geography and design and technology (including architecture).

Chapters 6 to 8 read somewhat as mini-encyclopaedias and are intended to be available to a teacher as a resource. They cannot fully attempt to provide detailed teaching approaches to the whole of school science! Anyway, many readers would not want such an approach, knowing that science education for a pluralist society is precisely the sort of science education where a single unified approach to the teaching of a particular topic for every conceivable audience cannot possibly succeed or even exist. Nevertheless, I am conscious that to give no indications as to how the material in these chapters could be used may be unhelpful. Accordingly, I have included a few examples of possible teaching strategies in an attempt to make concrete and specific some of my suggestions (and see the suggestions in Chapter 5). The sources I have used in these chapters are too many to list individually in these chapters. However, they are all given in the references and bibliography, the most extensively used being Ogilvie (1986), Millar *et al.* (1989) and Temple (1991).

Some thought was given to the most helpful way to arrange the material in these chapters. I was quite certain that I did not want to have a chapter on women's contributions, a chapter on contributions from China, one on contributions from Africa, etc. I did consider having one chapter on material suitable for 5–10-year-olds, one on material for 11–13-year-olds and one on material for 14–16-year-olds. In the end I rejected this approach partly because much of the material can be used over a wide range of ages. The arrangement I have adopted is a subject-specific one. It is approximately the case that Chapter 6 relates to biology, Chapter 7 to chemistry and Chapter 8 to physics. However, most readers will notice that I have in fact adopted the ordering of the 1991 Science National Curriculum for England and Wales (Department of Education and Science and the Welsh Office, 1991). The reasons for this are partly that many readers will be English or Welsh, and partly that this is a convenient way of ensuring that the earth sciences and astronomy are covered, without their enjoying full chapters. I have subdivided each of these chapters into the four or five strands defined by the National Curriculum Council (Department of Education and Science and the Welsh Office, 1991). Within each of these chapter sub-divisions material which relates mainly to younger pupils is placed early; that which relates to older pupils, later. I hope that these arrangements will make it as easy as possible for readers to find what they are looking for.

Chapter 9, 'The way forward', draws together the common threads of the whole book and points the way forward to better science education in schools. Finally, I have included a list of useful resources and a reference list and bibliography.

CHAPTER 2

What is science?

. . . I have found Ms . . . has had to deal with another problem: the history of science is almost entirely the history of *western* science, and Ms . . . has almost no knowledge of European history since classical times. This is obviously a considerable drawback in coming to a general view or coming to grips with many broader problems in the development of science . . .

(Copied from a 1981 end-of-term supervision report of a student from Pakistan doing the second-year undergraduate course in History of Science at Cambridge University)

This chapter is titled 'What is science?' because before we can go on to examine what sort of science education should be taking place in schools, we need to look at our understanding of science itself. I start from a consideration of the question 'Who are scientists?' and go on to examine the nature of science, but want to keep uppermost the issue of the pertinence of these questions for the teaching of science in schools.

Who are scientists?

Some months ago, I happened to see a new set of postage stamps produced in the UK, titled 'Scientific achievements' (issued 5 March 1991). It's worth spending a few moments imagining what you might expect (or hope!) to see on these stamps. Well, whatever you thought, the Royal Mail produced four stamps under the heading 'Scientific achievements' with the captions 'Faraday – Electricity', 'Babbage – Computer', 'Radar – Watson–Watt' and 'Jet Engine – Whittle' (Fig. 2.1). I find it difficult to imagine a narrower conception of what science is and who does it (Reiss, 1991). The image seems to be that real science is hard physics, with military applications, done by males who are white and worked on their own between about 1820 and 1940. No wonder so many students drop science at school as soon as

they have the chance! As over ten years of consistent research findings have told us, children come to school science lessons with clear impressions of what science is, how it operates and who does it (Driver *et al.*, 1985; Osborne and Freyberg, 1985; Scott *et al.*, 1987). There is a limit to what science teachers can realistically be expected to achieve in terms of challenging social perceptions and changing received wisdom.

It seems sad that the Royal Mail can produce a set of stamps that portrays such a biased view of science. One hopes that the next set of stamps to feature scientists will convey the notion that women do science, that science didn't start in the nineteenth century and finish around the time of the Second World War, that it isn't a Western construct, that it is done by people working in groups and that it permeates every area of life.

Countless examples could be given of the way we are all, including pupils and students in school, bombarded with messages about who scientists are, but two more will suffice. The first is taken from a book titled *History of Science* published in 1985 by the American Institute of Physics (Weart and Phillips, 1985). Some indication of the partiality of this publication is gleaned from the third sub-heading of the Introduction which modestly asserts 'History of modern science largely the history of physics'. Under this heading we read:

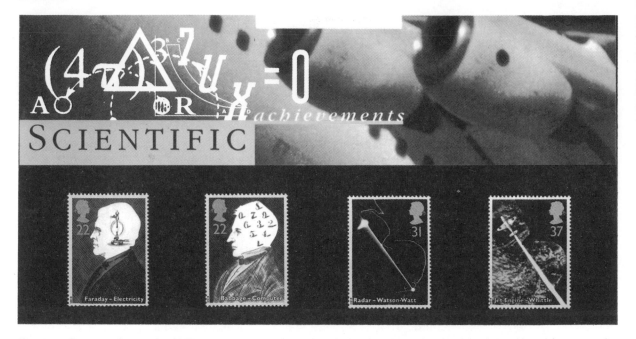

Fig. 2.1   Presentation pack of UK postage stamps issued on 5 March 1991 under the title 'Scientific achievements'.

Why was the history of modern science, so far as it has been written down, largely the history of physics? Perhaps it was for the same reasons that, ever since I. I. Rabi got together with Dwight Eisenhower, nearly all of the President's science advisers have been physicists. One reason might be that physics is a master-key to all the twentieth-century sciences; another, that nuclear weaponry has made scientists and the public especially watchful of physics; yet another, that physicists have often had broader viewpoints than other technically orientated people, with an interest in everything from music to social relations.

(Weart and Phillips, 1985: 2, of Introduction)

Unless you are from the USA *and* a physicist *and* have had a remarkably narrow education, it is unlikely that you will believe this. The worrying thing is that evidently a number of important and influential people really do believe that the history of modern science is largely the history of physics and that 'physicists have often had broader view-points than other technically oriented people'!

The second example of how we are all bombarded with messages about who scientists are comes from the recent broadcasting by the BBC World Service of a major series called 'They Made our World' (discussed by Reiss, 1993). To quote from the book that accompanies the series:

[The series was] broadcast around the world in 26 episodes Autumn 1990–Spring 1991. It features a gallery of great scientists, engineers, inventors and thinkers who contributed massively to the development of world [*sic*] we live in today.

(Hamilton, 1991, inside front cover)

One might have thought that a World Service series would at least have striven to be international in flavour, but the list of chapter titles is so distinctive that it is worth giving in full:

Sir Francis Bacon (1561–1626)
Sir Isaac Newton (1643–1747) [*sic*]
Joseph Priestley (1733–1804)
Antoine-Laurent Lavoisier (1743–1794)
Michael Faraday (1791–1867)
James Clerk Maxwell (1831–1879)
Sir Charles Lyell (1797–1875)
Charles Darwin (1809–1882)

Father Gregor Mendel (1822–1895)
Edward Jenner (1749–1823)
Louis Pasteur (1822–1895)
Sir Alexander Fleming (1881–1955)
James Watt (1736–1819)
George and Robert Stephenson (1781–1848)
   (1803–1859)
Sir Alexander Graham Bell (1847–1922)
Thomas Alva Edison (1847–1931)
Wilbur and Orville Wright (1867–1912) (1871–
   1948)
Henry Ford (1863–1947)
Professor Wilhelm Röntgen (1845–1923)
Guglielmo Marconi (1874–1937)
John Logie Baird (1888–1946)
Leo Hendrik Baekeland (1863–1944)
Alan Turing (1912–1954)
Albert Einstein (1879–1955)
Ernest Rutherford (1871–1937)
Robert Oppenheimer and the Manhattan Project
   (1904–1967)

Of the 28 people listed, none is a woman and none comes from outside Western Europe and the USA. Now the point I wish to make is that who a great scientist is partly depends on one's point of view. There are no absolute or universal criteria by which scientific excellence can infallibly be judged. It is all too easy for excellent scientists to be omitted from such lists. The Royal Mail, the contributors to *History of Physics* and the BBC World Service are guilty of sins of omission, rather than of commission. And, of course, what such people and institutions do is to reflect society's view of who scientists are. Powerful organizations such as the BBC and the Post Office reflect, perpetuate and even generate myths.

The effect that all this has can be seen by asking children to draw or describe a scientist. The results are consistent (Ward, 1986; Wyvill, 1991; Solomon, pers. comm.). Most scientists are portrayed as being white, male, middle-aged to old and wearing white coats (Fig. 2.2). To determine whether or not this is a distortion or an accurate reflection of the community of scientists, we need to go beyond the question 'Who are scientists?' and examine the nature of science.

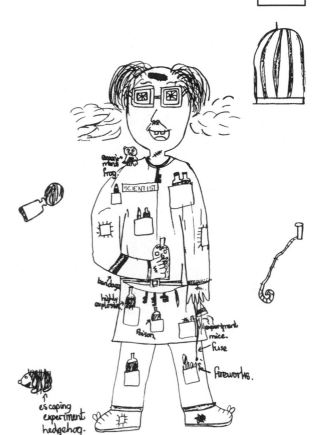

Fig. 2.2   A portrayal of a scientist by Caroline Allen (aged 9).

The nature of science

The popular view of what science is and how it proceeds probably goes something like this:

> Science consists of a body of knowledge about the world. The facts that comprise this knowledge are derived from accurate observations and careful experiments that can be checked by repeating them. As time goes on, scientific knowledge steadily progresses.

Such a view persists not only among the general public, but among science teachers and scientists despite the fact that it is held by most historians of science, philosophers of science, sociologists of science and science educationalists to be, at best, simplified and misleading and, at worst, completely erroneous (Collins, 1985; Latour, 1987;

Fig. 2.3 What is the relationship between science and that which it describes?

Fensham, 1988; Woolgar, 1988; Wellington, 1989; Harding, 1991).

It is not too much of a caricature to state that science is seen by many as *the* way to truth. Indeed, a number of important scientists have encouraged such a view by their writings and interviews (e.g. Peter Atkins and Richard Dawkins). It is generally assumed that the world 'out there' exists independently of the particular scientific methodology used to study it (Fig. 2.3). The advance of science then consists of scientists discovering eternal truths that exist independent of them and of the cultural context in which these discoveries are made. All areas of life are presumed amenable to scientific inquiry. Truth is supposed to emerge unambiguously from experiment like Pallas Athene, the goddess of wisdom, springing mature and unsullied from the head of Zeus. This view of science is mistaken for a number of reasons which I now want to go on to discuss.

Scientists have to choose on what to work

These choices are controlled partly by their background as individuals and partly by the values of the society in which they live and work. Most scientific research is not pure but applied. In particular, approximately a half of all scientific research funding is provided for military purposes. To give just one specific example of the way society determines on what scientists should work: the last ten years have seen a significant reduction in Great Britain of research into systematics, taxonomy and nomenclature (the classification, identification and naming of organisms). This is a direct result of changes in government funding which now, for instance, requires the Natural History Museum in London, the major UK centre for such research, to generate much of its own income. As a result, the number of scientists working there in these disciplines has more than halved as such scientists generate very little income.

Now, my point is not specifically to complain at the demise of systematics, taxonomy and nomenclature in the UK, but to point out that society and individual scientists have to choose on what to work. To a very large extent that choice is not determined on purely scientific criteria (if such criteria exist), but by political machinations and by the priorities (some would describe them as quirks) of funding bodies.

Scientists do not discover the world out there as it is

Scientists approach their topics of study with preconceptions. There is no such thing as an impartial observation. In the classroom this is seen to be the case every time a group of pupils is asked, for the first time, to draw some cells or sulphur crystals under the microscope. It isn't possible until you know what to draw. Unless you know that a leaf of pondweed consists of numerous small brick-like structures, all you *can* see is a mass of green with lines and occasional air bubbles. In the same way, the first time the German artist Dürer saw a rhinoceros, he drew what, by his normal standards, could be described as a fat armour-plated horse (Fig. 2.4). To expect pupils to draw regular epidermal cells the first time they see them is to expect more of them than Dürer could manage.

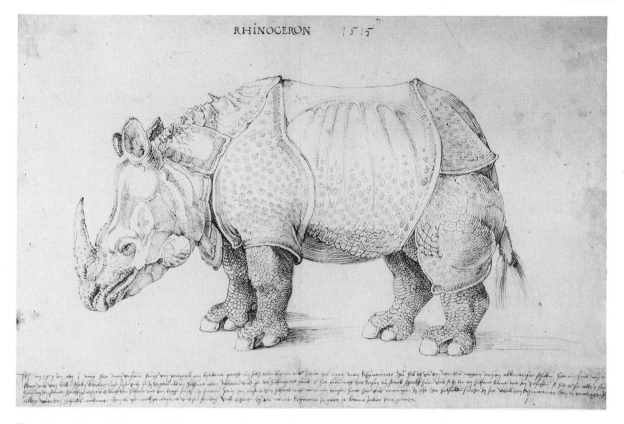

RHINOCERON 1515

Fig. 2.4 Albrecht Dürer's rhinoceros, Pen and Ink, 1515.

Instances where we can look back and see how scientists have unconsciously interpreted what they have seen in the light of their cultural heritage are legion. In his book *Metaphors of Mind*, Robert Sternberg points out that much of the present confusion surrounding the concept of intelligence stems from the variety of standpoints from which the human mind can be viewed (Sternberg, 1990; see also Eysenck and Kamin, 1981; Gould, 1981). The geographic metaphor is based on the notion that a theory of intelligence should provide a map of the mind. This view dates back at least to Gall, an early nineteenth century German anatomist and perhaps the most famous of phrenologists. Gall investigated the topography of the head, looking and feeling for tiny variations in the shape of the skull. According to Gall, a person's intelligence was to be discerned in the pattern of their cranial bumps. A second metaphor, the compu-

tational metaphor, envisions the mind as a computing device and analogizes the processes of the mind to the operations of a computer. Other metaphors discussed by Sternberg include the biological metaphor, the epistemological metaphor, the anthropological metaphor, the sociological metaphor and the systems metaphor. The point is that what scientists see and the models they construct to mirror reality depend very much on where their point of view is.

A clear example of how the work that scientists do is inevitably affected by who they are is provided by Jane Goodall's seminal (if that is not too sexist a term!) research on chimpanzee behaviour. When Jane Goodall first arrived to study the chimpanzees on the banks of Lake Tanganyika, the game warden who took her round made a mental note that she wouldn't last more than six weeks. She has stayed for over thirty years, producing the definitive accounts of chimpanzee social organization and behaviour in her fascinating and moving books *In the Shadow of Man* (van Lawick-Goodall, 1971) and *The Chimpanzees of Gombe: Patterns of Behavior* (Goodall, 1986).

An important point about Jane Goodall is that she had no formal training in ethology (the science of animal behaviour), having trained as a secretary after leaving school. As she herself wrote 'I was, of course, completely unqualified to undertake a scientific study of animal behaviour' (van Lawick-Goodall, 1971: 20). However, she spent some time with the celebrated palaeontologist Louis Leakey and his wife, Mary, on one of their annual expeditions to Olduvai Gorge on the Serengeti plains. Louis Leakey became convinced that Goodall was the person he had been looking for for twenty years – someone who was so fascinated by animals and their behaviour that they would be happy to spend at least two years studying chimpanzees in the wild. Leakey was particularly interested in the chimpanzees on the shore of Lake Tanganyika as the remains of prehistoric people had often been found on lake shores, and he thought it possible that an understanding of chimpanzee behaviour today might shed light on the behaviour of our Stone Age ancestors.

Goodall couldn't believe that Leakey was giving her the chance to do what she most wanted to do – watch chimpanzees in their natural habitat. She felt that her lack of training would disqualify her. But, as she later wrote:

> Louis, however, knew exactly what he was doing. Not only did he feel that a university training was unnecessary, but even that in some ways it might have been disadvantageous. He wanted someone with a mind uncluttered and unbiased by theory who would make the study for no other reason than a real desire for knowledge; and, in addition, someone with a sympathetic understanding of animal behaviour.
>
> (van Lawick-Goodall, 1971: 20)

Now the point, of course, is not that Jane Goodall could approach chimpanzees with a mind 'uncluttered and unbiased by theory' but that the clutter and theory in her mind was crucially distinct from that in someone who emerged from a university course in ethology. In the 1960s one of the great heresies of academic ethology was to be anthropomorphic – to treat non-humans as if they had human attributes and feelings. That is precisely what Jane Goodall did, and it allowed fundamentally new insights into chimpanzee behaviour. A flavour of Jane Goodall's approach can be obtained by reading the following quote:

> One day, when Flo was fishing for termites, it became obvious that Figan and Fifi, who had been eating termites at the same heap, were getting restless and wanted to go. But old Flo, who had already fished for two hours, and who was herself only getting about two termites every five minutes, showed no signs of stopping. Being an old female, it was possible that she might continue for another hour at least. Several times Figan had set off resolutely along the track leading to the stream, but on each occasion, after repeatedly looking back at Flo, he had given up and returned to wait for his mother.
>
> Flint, too young to mind where he was, pottered about on the heap, occasionally dabbling at a termite. Suddenly Figan got up again and this time approached Flint. Adopting the posture of a mother who signals her infant to climb on to her back, Figan bent one leg and reached back his hand to Flint, uttering a soft pleading whimper. Flint tottered up to him at once, and Figan, still whimpering, put his hand under Flint and gently pushed him on his back. Once Flint was safely aboard, Figan, with another quick glance at Flo, set off rapidly along the track. A moment later Flo discarded her tool and followed.
>
> (van Lawick-Goodall, 1971: 114–5)

Other writers at the time did not give names to their animals; nor did they use language like 'getting restless', 'wanted to go', 'set off resolutely' and 'pottered about'; nor did they impute to their subjects the ability consciously to manipulate one another.

Apart from her lack of formal training, there is another factor about Jane Goodall that may well be significant. She is a woman. The three longest-running studies on animal behaviour have all been carried out by women: Jane Goodall on chimpanzees (1960 to present); Dian Fossey on gorillas (1966 to 1985 when she was murdered, probably because of her dedication to the gorillas (Mowat, 1987)); and Fiona Guinness on red deer (1972 to present (see Clutton-Brock *et al.*, 1982)). All three worked/work quite exceptionally long hours with what can only be described as total dedication. In 1978 and 1979 I spent a couple of months working alongside Fiona Guinness. On average she worked 14 hours a day, seven days a week.

My point is not that research scientists ought to work this long, nor that only women can show the empathy with animals that these three did or do. Rather, it is that the personal and social pressures that shaped Jane Goodall, Dian Fossey and Fiona Guinness were crucial to the type of science that they carried out or do carry out. *And this is true for all scientists*. It's just that it is easier to see in these three cases. Donna Haraway in her book *Primate Visions: Gender, Race and Nature in the World of Modern Science* argues that scientific practice is story-telling. The work that primatologists do is moulded by the environment in which they operate and by the sort of people they are, so that the stories that primatologists tell reflect the social agendas that surround them (Gowaty, 1991).

A final example of how societal pressures and assumptions can significantly affect the conclusions reached by scientists is afforded by the work of Tinbergen and Ter Pelkwijk (Ter Pelkwijk and Tinbergen 1937; Tinbergen, 1951). This classic story is frequently given in school and university textbooks to illustrate courtship, territorial behaviour and reproduction. It goes as follows:

> In spring, male sticklebacks acquire territories from which they chase away intruders of either sex. During this period males acquire red bellies. This redness makes males particularly likely to chase away other males. Tinbergen found that a realistically shaped but non-red model provoked little interest, whereas extremely crude models painted red on their lower surfaces provoked strong aggression from the territorial male. The male finishes building a nest and now becomes interested in females swollen with eggs. When a female appears he swims towards her in a curious zig-zag fashion (the zig-zag dance). When she sees him the female responds by swimming towards him with her head and tail turned upwards, thereby displaying her swollen abdomen. The male then leads the female and shows her his nest entrance by poking it with his snout. She enters his nest and the male gives her rump several prods with a trembling motion, and this stimulates her to lay eggs. When she has discharged her eggs, she leaves the nest and the male enters it, ejaculates over the eggs and fertilises them. He then chases the female away. Altogether he may mate with as many as five different females. Having fertilised a certain number of clutches, the male loses his readiness to court females. Instead he begins regular ventilation of the eggs by fanning them. Fanning serves to provide the eggs with oxygen and continues until they hatch.

This elegant story is backed by a fifteen-minute film made by Oxford Scientific Films. Notice how the male stickleback is at the centre of the stage, with a crowd of passive females waiting around to be directed and prodded. Recent studies, however, have significantly changed the story (Li and Owings, 1978; Ridley and Rechten, 1981; Rowland, 1982; Reiss, 1984).

For our purposes the work done by Li and Owings is most significant. The crucial factor in Li and Owings' work was that, unlike previous researchers, they spent as much time watching female as male sticklebacks. Furthermore, before individuals of either sex were introduced to individuals of the other sex, the sexes were sexually segregated in groups of six. This enabled Li and Owings to determine female–female interactions as well as male–male interactions. Their results contrast with the popular notion that female sticklebacks are relatively passive participants in reproduction.

Female sticklebacks averaged 50 per cent *more* aggressive encounters per hour in the all-female group than the males did in the all-male groups. The lesser aggression of the males was not due to any abnormal behaviour on their part: the density of males used was that recommended by previous researchers and males set up and defended territories, as usual, in the experiments. In the all-female groups, females were kept at the same density as males had been. Some females defended territories, others did not. On three occasions females actually lost their eggs. This was observed twice. On each occasion a more dominant female poked or squashed a more subordinate female, and repeated pressure led to the two subordinate females prematurely shedding their eggs.

Li and Owings also studied groups consisting of six females and six males. Female–female interactions were also important in this situation. On three occasions a subordinate female accepted a courting male before the dominant. Each time the dominant disrupted courtship. On the two occasions that a subordinate female attempted to disrupt courtship by a dominant female, the attempts failed.

It is possible to suppose from the above examples that only bad science is affected by the presuppositions of the individuals that carry it out, influenced by the hidden assumptions of the society in which they live and move and have their being. Indeed, most practising scientists are happy with the notion that this is the case. However, many sociologists of science want to go much further than this. They argue that every science inevitably reflects the interests, the values, the unconscious suppositions and the beliefs of the society that gives rise to it (Feyerabend, 1988; Longino, 1990). For an example of how even what is almost universally acknowledged as being among the best of science may have critically been influenced by what might be described as extra-scientific forces, consider some of Newton's thinking in his *Principia* (Freudenthal, 1986; discussed by Chalmers, 1990).

One of Newton's key advances was to argue that the properties of wholes are to be explained in terms of the essential properties of their parts. For instance, Newton asserted that the extension, hardness, impenetrability, mobility and force of inertia of the whole result from the extension, hardness, impenetrability, mobility and force of inertia of the parts. From this he concluded that the smallest of particles are also all extended, hard, impenetrable, moveable and endowed with their proper forces of inertia.

Newton's assertion that the whole is simply the sum of its component parts provided the crucial foundation stone for his pivotal work on gravity, but from where did he get the idea? The assertion, cannot, of course, be proved. Indeed, every biolo-

gist knows that the properties of an organism (say, a giraffe) cannot be deduced from the properties of the molecules of which it is comprised. Biology is all about understanding that the properties that one level of organization has are not necessarily apparent from studying lower levels of organization.

Freudenthal traces Newton's assumptions back to the individualistic understanding of society that emerged in the seventeenth century as European feudal society became replaced by early forms of capitalist society. Freudenthal points out that while the various new conceptions of society formulated in the seventeenth century by Thomas Hobbes, John Locke and others differ from each other in significant respects, they have one thing in common. They all attempt to explain society by reference to the properties of the individuals that make up the society. Further, individuals are assumed to have these properties independently of their existence in society.

At this point it may be worth pointing out that accepting the essential premise of sociologists of science that science and society are inevitably, inexorably intertwined, does not necessarily require one to abandon all belief in the objectivity of science. As Alan Chalmers puts it: 'The natural world does not behave in one way for capitalists and in another way for socialists, in one way for males and another for females, in one way for Western cultures and another for Eastern cultures' (Chalmers, 1990: 112). This seems reasonable. However, a scientist's *perceptions* of the natural world, as well as her interpretations, come through her senses, herself as a person and her culture. What is of significance for science education is that there can be no single, universal, acultural science. Rather, every sort of science is an ethnoscience, as I shall now go on to argue.

Science as a collection of ethnosciences

The term 'ethnoscience' first became widely used in the anthropological literature of the 1960s (Bulmer, 1971). It has been used in two ways:

> It refers firstly to the 'science', in the sense of modes of classification of the material and social

universe, possessed by societies unaffected or little affected by modern international scientific thinking and discoveries. Secondly, it refers to a particular anthropological approach which has as its objective the systematic 'scientific' investigation of ways in which particular societies classify the universe . . .

(Bulmer, 1971: 22)

There is much that such ethnoscientific research has contributed which is of value to those hoping to fashion a science education for a pluralist society, but we need to broaden this definition slightly. To restrict the term 'ethnoscience' to societies 'unaffected . . . by modern international scientific thinking and discoveries' is both to misunderstand the nature of science, and to risk adopting a patronising and racist attitude to such ethnosciences. It misunderstands the nature of science because, as I have argued above, *all* science is set in a cultural milieu, so that we cannot validly distinguish a number of ethnosciences from a single international non-ethnoscientific science. It risks being patronising and racist because accepting such a definition of ethnoscience inevitably makes it likely that a writer, however impressed she or he is with a particular ethnoscience, ends up comparing it with 'modern international scientific thinking and discoveries' which then act as a benchmark against which the particular ethnoscience is judged.

Further, we should not assume that within a particular society, all scientific thinking operates within the same paradigm. By virtue of differences between individuals in such important characteristics as gender, religious beliefs, ethnicity, age and disability, individuals may differ significantly in their scientific understanding and conception of the world. There are two extreme ways in which a teacher may react to such differences. The more common is to adopt, implicitly, what we can call a 'deficit' model of science. Here all inter-individual (and inter-cultural) differences in scientific understanding and practice are held to exist because individuals and cultures differ in the extent to which they understand and practise the one, true science. The role of a science teacher is clearly then to remove obstacles to the understanding of this single true science, and then teach it (cf. Layton *et al.*, 1986; Layton, 1991).

The second extreme way in which a teacher could react to inter-individual and inter-cultural differences in scientific understanding and practice is to adopt what we can call an 'all sciences are equal' model. Here there is no objectivity in science. All scientific methodologies and findings, however much they differ, are of equal validity.

I suspect it is because this second model leads to conclusions which, to practically every science teacher, are so manifestly absurd, that the first model – with its assumptions of the one, true science – is so often adopted. What I will attempt to argue is that there is a middle ground between these two models, a middle ground which genuinely allows for inter-individual and inter-cultural differences without abandoning all claims to real scientific progress.

Published or be damned

Once a scientist or group of scientists has discovered something or produced a new model to interpret a phenomenon, it is necessary for their work to be disseminated in some form, usually through publication. Getting work published, read, recognized and cited depends greatly on the personalities of individuals involved and on what society values.

As a single example of the importance of society's world view in accepting a scientific theory, consider the circumstances that surrounded the publication of William Harvey's ideas on the circulation of the blood. Although the circulation of the blood had been established in China by the second century BCE at the latest, in Europe the idea was proposed by Michael Servetus (1546), Realdo Colombo (1559), Andrea Cesalpino (1571) and Giordano Bruno (1590). These men had read of the circulation of the blood in the writings of an Arab of Damascus, Ibn Nafis (died 1288) who himself seems to have obtained at least some of his ideas from China (Temple, 1991). Harvey published his 'discovery' in 1628. It is possible that the early seventeenth century accounts of a huge diversity of pumping engines for mine drainage and water supply caused the scientific community and general public to be in an appropriate frame of mind to accept the notion of the heart as a mechanical pump (cf. Russell, 1988). In other words, most people remember Harvey as the person responsible for the discovery of the circulation of the blood because earlier proponents of the idea published them at times when their understanding and acceptance was more difficult for people.

Mention can also be made of the importance of the language that scientists use. Some scientists are simply much better at writing their work up so that it is more likely to be published, read and cited. What people then remember is the language used as well as the science. Indeed, the two cannot be separated. We cannot sift out the language of corruption to reveal a pure, unsullied science.

A clear illustration of the intimacy of the relationship between language and science was provided by the attempts of newspapers and magazines in the UK on 24 April 1992 to describe the reported discovery by a NASA satellite of radiation from the Big Bang. The word most often used was 'ripple'. The first two paragraphs of *The Independent* report (which dominated the front page of the paper) were as follows:

> Fourteen thousand million years ago the universe hiccuped. Yesterday, American scientists announced that they may have heard the echo.
>
> A Nasa spacecraft has detected ripples at the edge of the Cosmos which are the fossilised imprint of the birth of the stars and galaxies around us today.

Even *The Sun* weighed in. Under a headline 'We find secret of the creation' (page 6) the ripples were said to 'look like wispy clouds'. The publicity attending the news was heightened by Stephen Hawking who was reported on the front page of the *Daily Mail* as describing the finding as 'the discovery of the century, if not of all time'. In fact, as is often the case with scientific discoveries, the reported interpretation of the findings has been challenged and another one proposed (summarized in non-technical language by Chown, 1992).

It's easy to make fun of reports which talk of wispy clouds and the universe hiccuping, but my point is that all science has to be reported in a language, even if it is the language of mathematics. And all languages, including the language(s) of mathematics, are human constructs.

Changing conceptions of science

The notion as to what constitutes science differs over time and between cultures (Hiatt and Jones, 1988; Brooke, 1991). Attempts by certain historians and philosophers of science to identify a distinctive 'scientific method' which demarcates science absolutely from other disciplines have not proved successful. Though certain principles, such as testability and repeatability, may be central to modern science, it is now widely held that the question 'What is science?' can only be answered 'That which is recognized as such by a scientific community'. Although this answer, being somewhat tautologous, may appear distinctly unhelpful, its truth may be seen by examining what other times and cultures include in science.

Figure 2.5 shows the early classification of Islamic science. To many readers the inclusion of such things as syntax, grammar, pronunciation, poetry, Metaphysics, jurisprudence and rhetoric may appear surprising. But one should remember that throughout the Middle Ages, Western philosophy operated within a framework of the seven liberal arts. These consisted of the verbal arts (the trivium) – grammar, rhetoric and logic or dialectic – and the mathematical quadrivium – arithmetic, music, geometry and astronomy (Wagner, 1983). The twentieth century Western understanding of science is just that – a twentieth century Western understanding. In particular, school science is all too often seen as being absolutely distinct from other domains of knowledge such as the creative arts and economics despite the fact that practising scientists, historians and philosophers of science agree that creativity and financial constraints are of prime importance in science.

Science is also often seen in conflict with religion despite the fact that other models of the relationship between science and religion exist and many

Science of language
syntax
grammar
pronunciation and speech
poetry

Logic
necessary conditions for premises which would lead
    in a syllogism to certain knowledge
definitions of useful syllogisms and the means of
    discovering dialectical proofs
examination of errors in proofs
definition of oratory
study of poetry

Propaedeutic sciences
arithmetic
geometry
optics
science of the heavens
music
science of weights
science of tool-making

Physics and Metaphysics

Physics
knowledge of the principles which underlie natural
    bodies
knowledge of the nature and character of the elements
science of the generation and corruption of bodies
science of the reactions which the elements undergo
    in order to form compounds
science of compound bodies formed of the four
    elements
science of minerals
science of plants
science of animals

Metaphysics
knowledge of the essence of beings
knowledge of the principles of the particular and
    observational sciences
knowledge of noncorporeal beings, leading finally to
    the knowledge of the Truth, that is, of God, one of
    whose names is the Truth

Science of Society
jurisprudence
rhetoric

Fig. 2.5 The early classification of the sciences
according to the Iḥṣā' al-'ulūm of al-Fārābī.

outstanding scientists have a religious faith (Peacocke, 1979; Polkinghorne, 1983; Barbour, 1990; Poole, 1990c; Wilkinson, 1990; Brooke, 1991). Whether science teachers should teach the relationship between science and religion is discussed in Chapter 5 in the context of teaching controversial issues.

Much school science operates on the assumption that 'real science' consists in doing laboratory experiments to test hypotheses. I should like to relate an anecdote to illustrate this. When I started teaching social biology to 16–19-year-olds, the Examinations Board that set the syllabus included a project. One of my students was a very fit athlete who lived in Bahrain out of term time. He carried out on himself measurements of such physiological variables as body temperature and body mass just before and just after completing a number of runs of predetermined distance both in the UK and in Bahrain. Another student was interested to see whether a person's astrological sign (determined by their birth date) correlated with their choice of school subjects (e.g. sciences versus humanities) or with their personality. Accordingly she carried out a large survey of fellow students. The Examinations Board marked its projects on a 1 (top) to 9 (bottom) scale. Both students were given a 9 which meant that their project contributed nothing to their overall mark: in other words it was scored zero, their projects being deemed to have had no scientific worth.

I'm not claiming that either of these projects was the finest I have ever seen. But I am convinced that the marks they were given (and these marks were not changed on appeal) reflected too narrow an assumption in the Examiners' minds about what constituted a scientific project.

In England and Wales, the Science National Curriculum (Department of Education and Science and the Welsh Office, 1991) Attainment Target 1 'Scientific Investigation' has a model of science which, while there is much that is good about it, would disqualify, for instance, much of the work done by astronomers, taxonomists, palaeontologists and theoreticians from being included within its compass. Mayr has argued that after the time of the Middle Ages (in Western

Europe) the physical sciences were the paradigm of science:

> As everyone was willing to concede, the universality and predictability that seemed to characterize studies of the inanimate world were missing from biology. Because life was restricted to the earth, as far as anyone knew, any statements and generalizations one could make concerning living organisms would seem to be restricted in space and time. To make matters worse, such statements nearly always seemed to have exceptions. Explanations usually were not based on universal laws but rather were pluralistic. In short the theories of biology violated every canon of 'true science', as the philosophers had derived them from the methods and principles of classical physics.
>
> (Mayr, 1988: 9)

Sadly, it is still the case that much school science has too narrow an understanding of the *methods* of science. This, I suspect, is one reason why pupils too often find their school science unsatisfying. They know that it's too restricted a way of looking at the world. And they're right.

CHAPTER 3

Science curricula for a pluralist society

L.   From Shakhimardan to Vuadil it is three hours on foot, while to Fergana it is six hours. How much time does it take to go on foot from Vuadil to Fergana?

K.   No, it's six hours from Vuadil to Fergana. You're wrong . . . it's far and you wouldn't get there in three hours.

L.   That makes no difference; a teacher gave this problem as an exercise. If you were a student, how would you solve it?

K.   But how do you travel – on foot or horseback?

L.   It's all the same – well, let's say on foot.

K.   No, then you won't get there! It's a long way . . . if you were to leave now, you'd get to Vuadil very, very late in the evening.

(A conversation between A. R. Luria (L.), of the Institute of Psychology at Moscow University, and Kamrak (K.), a 36-year-old peasant from a remote village in the region of Uzbekistan and Kirghizia in 1931–32. Taken from Luria (1976: 129))

In this chapter I look at the sort of science that should be being taught in schools. I will start by assuming that the central message of Chapter 2 has been accepted, namely that there is no single, acultural science.

Science curricula worldwide

When we look at different science curricula in different countries, one fact stands out. They are generally very similar. In 1984 a questionnaire about the place of science and technology in school timetables was sent to all 161 member states of Unesco. Replies were received from 97 countries and these, together with in-depth follow-up studies of selected countries, were analysed and published (Morris, 1990). Combining the results of the Unesco study with the work of others on science curricula (Davis, 1979; Al-Faruqi and Nasseef, 1981; Ingle and Turner, 1981; Ogawa, 1986; Amara, 1987; Fensham, 1988; Hewson, 1988; George and Glasgow, 1989; Vlaardinger-broek, 1990; Shaharir bin Mohamad Zain, 1991) the following conclusions can be summarized:

- Most countries base their school science courses on ones imported from Europe or the USA. Indeed, a number of countries teach science in English even though this is not the first home language for many of the pupils.
- Such imported courses often make unrealistic assumptions about the available provision of school science equipment and about the depth of formal scientific training that teachers have had.
- Imported courses inhibit more appropriate local developments.
- Especially at primary level, courses that attempt to stress the processes of science, with a reduced emphasis on the content of science, often run into difficulties. This is partly because of the lack of confidence and knowledge of formal science that teachers at this level almost universally have, and partly because what is taught in such courses does not seem either to the teachers or to the parents of the pupils to be 'real science'.
- At best, courses that ignore indigenous science result in pupils learning school science, but simultaneously retaining their understanding of traditional science. In a school setting, school

science may be used, but out of the classroom this is less likely to be the case.

An instructive example of a well-established education programme where care has been taken to ensure its relevance and applicability for the target population is provided by the Namutamba Project in Uganda (Morris, 1990). The Namutamba Project was introduced shortly after Uganda gained independence. Its overarching aim was to provide an education programme relevant to a country in which 90 per cent of the population lives in rural areas. Its specific aims are to:

1 Attempt to check the exodus of rural school leavers to towns and cities through the provision of sound experiences in general education, pre-vocational and vocational education.
2 Ensure a complete primary education cycle to the greater number of children.
3 Introduce new curriculum content, teaching methods and materials in the primary schools and in pre-service and in-service teacher training.
4 Undertake or strengthen post-primary services of pre-vocational and vocational skills.
5 Provide functional literacy, general education, craft work, nutrition and health education for youth and adults, men and women.
6 Collect data on those factors which are likely to impede or to facilitate education in its task of providing integrated rural development.
7 Provide data and information which may make it possible for other countries facing similar problems to benefit from Uganda's experience of the project.

(Morris, 1990: 202)

In the Namutamba Project, the following science units are covered in primary school:

Our environment:
    animals and plants in the school compound
Changes in our environment:
    natural and man-made changes in animals, plants, the sky, etc.
Crop husbandry:
    soil, planting, caring, harvesting, storage and marketing the common crops of Uganda

Pests and diseases
Animal husbandry:
    housing, feeding and caring for domestic animals, their products, their diseases
Our health and keeping healthy:
    the importance of sanitation
Study of the system of the mammals:
    e.g. skeletal, muscular, digestive, circulatory, respiratory
Bacteria and disease:
    identification, symptoms, causes, effect, control, prevention and treatment of common diseases in Uganda
Air, water and weather:
    properties, use and measurement
Food and nutrition:
    collecting, preparing, storage and use of different types of foods, malnutrition diseases
Study of the flowering plant:
    general structure and functions of roots, stems, leaves, flowers and seeds
Measurement:
    measuring regularly shaped objects, calculating volume, weighing objects in air
Matter, work and energy:
    matter and its states
Forms of energy:
    heat, sound, light, electricity, magnetism
Simple machines:
    levers and applications of simple machines
Rocks and minerals:
    use of rocks and minerals of Uganda
Home and family life:
    growth and development, family relationships
Safety and accident prevention/first aid
Classification of living things:
    plant and animal kingdom

It should be mentioned that English is the official language in all schools and government communications.

Another example of an attempt to provide a science education programme tailored for the needs of the pupils in that particular country is provided by the Science Aotearoa initiative in Aotearoa (New Zealand). This scheme is still in its early stages. It is intended that:

attention will be focused on New Zealand's natural environment (the bush, the sea, the mountains and volcanoes); Maori names will be employed; Maori folk science, horticulture and technology, and the engineering of the early settlers, will be studied; the exploitation and utilization of local materials (greenstone, ironsand, gold, Kauri timber, flax) will be described; and an attempt will be made to develop an alternative view of the nature and purpose of science and technology that is more in keeping with traditional Maori views concerning the fundamental unity between humanity and nature.

(Hodson, 1990: 106)

Assumptions about what should be learned in science may be culturally specific

Here are two examples where attempts to transfer one set of scientific concepts or facts from one culture to another have not proved successful.

Aboriginal nutrition

Sandra Stacy worked with Aboriginal people in Northern and Central Australia as a community health nurse (Stacy, 1983). White people working in remote parts of Australia with traditionally oriented Aboriginals have known for many years that the physical health of the Aboriginal people has been significantly poorer than that of the rest of the Australian community. Much of this has been perceived as being due to what are seen as high rates of respiratory disease, diarrhoea and undernutrition among infants, all too often resulting in illness and death. White health workers have felt that these conditions could be prevented, and that teaching about infant nutrition would be a necessary part of such a preventative programme.

For many years white health educators had attempted to teach Aboriginals about the relationship between food and health, about the nutritional needs of infants, about the differing nutrient values of foods, and about practical aspects of budgeting, food storage and food preparation. However, to little discernible effect.

Stacy worked with Aboriginals from the Pitjantjatjara language groups who live in the desert country of central Australia. Teaching was done in the Pitjantjatjara language, both in Alice Springs and in the bush. After four years it was found that although those who participated in the courses could repeat accurately the facts they had been taught *and* perform appropriate tasks, there was no indication that any of this learning was used in their day-to-day lives. Further research showed that the white health workers and the Aboriginals saw foods in quite distinct ways. The white health workers saw foods in terms of the nutrients they contain; the Aboriginals saw foods in terms of their significance for human relationships. As Stacy puts it:

> From my point of view, no matter how the subject of food was introduced, be it traditional or European food, sooner or later, and usually sooner, the Aboriginals would turn the subject round to their relatives. It was very frustrating for me, and in retrospect I realise it must have been equally frustrating for them.
> Because I saw food in terms of nutrients, I didn't hear them saying they saw it in terms of relationships. Because they saw food in terms of relationships, they did not hear what I was saying about nutrients.

(Stacy, 1983: 139)

Stacy concluded that the Aboriginals chose to participate in the programme because they saw it as an opportunity to make friends with white Australians. The relationships were the end in themselves. For Stacy and her co-workers the establishment of good relationships with the Aboriginals had been a means to an end, the end being improved infant physical health.

Nigerian traditional cosmology and students' acquisition of a science process skill

Olugbemiro Jegede and Peter Okebukola investigated the interaction between traditional beliefs about living organisms and the precision with which students described their observations about these organisms (Jegede and Okebukola, 1991). A total of 319 pre-degree science students (151 females; 168 males) with a mean age of 16.9 years in a Nigerian university were studied. Each student was assessed on a scale which measured their belief in traditional cosmology. Each student was also assessed on their observational skills of ten biological phenomena. For example, students were asked to observe and note the colour changes in a chameleon in a cage in the laboratory and also to describe in full what happens when a leaf of the sensitive plant *Mimosa pudica* is touched.

Jegede and Okebukola found that students with a high level of belief in African traditional cosmology made significantly fewer correct scientific observations of biological structures and processes when compared with those students with a low level of belief. This is what one would expect, as the biological items were chosen because of the particular traditional beliefs associated with them. For example, among students with a high level of belief in African traditional cosmology, a chameleon portends an ominous event on being seen, while touching *Mimosa pudica* is associated with the imminent loss of one's grandfather. What I would like to suggest is that presumably the choice of a set of biological specimens which interacted *positively* with traditional beliefs might have led to significantly *more* correct scientific observations.

The performance of minorities in school science lessons

From a reading of the above it might be thought that minorities always do less well in schools. This, of course, is far from the case. Some minorities perform, on average, poorer than those belonging to the majority culture; some minorities perform, on average, better than those belonging to the majority culture (e.g. Table 3.1).

Precisely why different minorities differ so considerably in their school performance is still controversial. Early studies looked at why minorities often underachieve and emphasized that the education provided for such groups is all too often inappropriate (reviewed by Foley, 1991; see also Whitelegg, 1992). For example, education may be provided only in a second language; the curricu-

Table 3.1 Percentage of pupils achieving five or more CSE grade 1 or O levels (grades A, B or C) in 1985 in the 72 per cent of Inner London Education Authority schools which provided information on examination success for 16-year-olds as a function of ethnic background (after Kysel, 1988).

Ethnic background	5+ CSE 1 or O (A–C)	Number of pupils
African	10.3	426
African Asian	24.7	162
Arab	6.6	91
Bangladeshi	4.2	333
Caribbean	4.6	2 981
E/S/W/I*	10.3	10 685
Greek	11.5	243
Indian	26.4	398
Pakistani	17.7	231
S. E. Asian	17.0	300
Turkish	2.6	268
Other	18.0	940
All	10.2	17 058

* English, Scottish, Welsh and Irish.

lum may be sexist or racist; or the teaching may favour one style of learning. There is no doubt that such explanations account for much underachievement by minority groups. (I include girls here within the categorization of 'minority group' on the grounds that although numerically not rarer than boys, girls are usually in a minority with respect to the attention they receive and the power they wield.)

Although the argument that much of the education received by minority groups is inappropriate, whether in science or elsewhere, is valid, it fails to account for the considerable differences that exist between different minority groups in educational achievement (e.g. Table 3.1). Why is it, for instance, that in the USA some ethnic minorities who are culturally and linguistically very different from the majority of their teachers (e.g. Chinese, Punjabi) have none of the learning problems associated with other minorities (e.g. African Americans, Mexican Americans and Native Americans)?

In 1981, John Ogbu suggested an answer. He argued that those minorities that do well simply do not perceive the racial barriers and the resulting lack of opportunities for certain groups in American society (Ogbu, 1981). This is particularly the case with recent immigrant groups that have chosen to come to the USA (e.g. from China and Pakistan). It is the *involuntary* minority groups (e.g. Native Americans, African Americans) who underachieve. Further, such underachievement (and this is equally true of girls in physical science lessons and of working-class pupils in almost any school), can result from minorities being faced with a choice: abandon your cultural distinctiveness and do well academically *or* retain your cultural distinctiveness and fail academically. I imagine that Ogbu's analysis will be convincing to many science teachers who are all-too-familiar with the observation that for certain of their pupils to succeed academically is, depressingly, for them to risk social ostracism.

There are only really two ways out of this disheartening scenario in which significant groups of pupils are, albeit subconsciously, opting out of school science lessons. The first is to assume that the fault lies with pupils' perceptions that there is a clash between school science and their culture. Given this assumption, the best course of action is to attempt to encourage pupils to continue with the existing curriculum.

The second course of action is to admit that much of the science education presently delivered in schools assumes a male, white, middle-class perspective, and therefore tends to appeal most to male, white, middle-class pupils. Given this admission, the question then is whether this is an inevitable characteristic of science, or whether science teaching can be changed to appeal to a wider audience. It is, of course, the argument of this book that not only can science teaching be changed to appeal to a wider audience, but that such a change will result in better science education *per se*.

What is the intended purpose of school science?

Fundamentally, school science can have one of two aims. The first is to ensure that the next generation of scientists receives an appropriate school science education. This is a top–down model of school science education in that syllabuses and assessment procedures serve to ensure that the right number of people with the right qualifications and grasp of science go on to study it in Higher Education.

The second possible aim of school science is to ensure that all pupils are scientifically literate. This means providing a science education so that both in school, and once they leave it, people bring their knowledge and understanding of science (both its methodology and content) to bear on everyday issues. Questions generated by such everyday issues might include 'Should we install double glazing?'; 'Is it safe to eat raw eggs?' and 'Should I press my local council to install bottle banks?'.

The two aims are not incompatible, but neither are they fully compatible. In most countries at most times the first aim has had precedence (Fensham, 1988; Chapman, 1991; Jenkins, 1992) despite the fact that most attempts to define the purpose of education end up referring to the benefits to individuals, not to society.

I will take it as read that science education should be for the benefit of all individuals. In this sense, I am anti-élitist. However, I am sufficient of an optimist to believe that it is possible to provide a science education that, while focusing on the needs of individuals, will ultimately benefit society too.

What is school science?

An objection often raised against the sort of science education I am advocating in this book is that it isn't really concerned with real science, but rather with the peripheries of science – with technology, with history, with geography and with social studies. Once we forget, so the argument goes, about things like electricity generators (which should be done in technology), who discovered certain scientific principles and facts (history), human population growth (geography) and issues like intelligence and race (social studies), science teachers can be left to get on with real science – things like atoms and gravity and DNA.

Chapter 2, on the nature of science, and this chapter, about the purpose of school science, should answer these objections, but here I want to make a different point. As soon as we start to consider how scientific knowledge impinges on the real world and on human lives we enter the contentious area of ethics and values. Some would rather such questions could be avoided in science education, believing that science is value-free. However, the view that science is value-free is tenable only if our definition of science is unbelievably narrow (see Head, 1985; Gosling and Musschenga, 1985; Frazer and Kornhauser, 1986; Midgley, 1992; Solomon , 1992; Poole, in press).

School science teaching should enable all pupils to understand the natural world in which they live. We must consider pupils' existing knowledge for two reasons. First, teaching formal school science in ignorance of a pupil's prior understanding may lead to little real learning. It may result in a pupil having a veneer of formal scientific understanding over a deeper mass of traditional knowledge. Such a veneer is all too easily rubbed off once the school classroom is left. But secondly, and just as importantly, it must *not* be assumed, implicitly or explicitly, that all traditional scientific understanding is fallacious and needs eradicating before 'real' scientific learning can take place. Just as every good language teacher starts from what language knowledge, understanding and skills a pupil already possesses, so must science teachers.

The intended, implemented and attained science curriculum

When considering science curricula, a useful distinction can be made between the intended, the implemented and the attained science curriculum. (I am grateful to Alan Bishop for drawing this distinction to my attention.) These have been defined as follows:

> By the Intended Curriculum is meant the curriculum as planned at the national, provincial, or local levels by curriculum committees and consultants, and as codified in curriculum guides. The Implemented Curriculum is the curriculum as contained in the various texts and materials which are selected and approved for use in the schools and as communicated by teachers in their classrooms. The Attained Curriculum is the curriculum as learned and assimilated by students.
>
> (Robitaille and Dirks, 1982: 17)

What we are interested in, of course, is the attained curriculum. Attempts to reform the curriculum all too often assume that changes in the implemented, or even the intended, curriculum will result in changes in the attained curriculum. They usually don't. To change the attained curriculum requires both teacher and learner to internalize the new curriculum. Quite a tall order!

Why aren't there more black/women scientists featured in school textbooks?

The reader who has gone along with most of what I have already written might still say: 'Well, yes, I can see what you're going on about. But it won't make much difference to my teaching. After all I'm still going to teach Newton's laws and Mendeléev's periodic table and Darwin's theory of natural selection. I can't pretend that they were discovered by women or black scientists.' Or as a physics educator once said to me: 'Once you've put up the posters of Marie Curie and Dorothy Hodgkin, what then?'

Part of the aim of Chapters 6, 7 and 8 is to enrich such science teachers' teaching so that they can incorporate a greater diversity of examples into their teaching, but there is more to pluralistic science teaching than that. A pluralist science teacher will employ a pupil-centred approach and will cover certain topics and issues in her science lessons that would either be omitted by most other science teachers or treated differently (see Chapters 4 and 5).

Nevertheless, the question 'Why aren't there more black/women scientists featured in school textbooks?' is an important one and one that should perhaps explicitly be addressed at some point in a pupil's science education. I can think of four main reasons.

Ignorance on the part of the writers of the textbooks of the part played by particular women and black scientists

Often writers of school science textbooks do not realize the role played by women or black scientists. To give just one example, the English doctor Edward Jenner is almost universally credited with the invention of vaccination as a way of avoiding smallpox in 1796. Yet the practice of inoculation against smallpox was successfully being practised in China in the tenth century CE and in Greece, Turkey, India and parts of Arabia over a hundred years before the practice reached England (Smith, 1987; Temple, 1991). Inoculation against smallpox was first reported in England in 1701 but was popularized by Lady Mary Wortley Montagu who went to Turkey with her husband, the new Ambassador, in 1716. In a letter to Miss Mary Chiswell, April 1717, she described what she had seen:

> The small-pox, so fatal, and so general amongst us, is here entirely harmless by the invention of *ingrafting*, which is the term they give it . . . People send to one another to know if any of their family has a mind to have the small-pox: they make parties for this purpose, and when they are met (commonly fifteen or sixteen together), the old woman comes with a nut-shell full of the matter of the best sort of smallpox, and asks what veins you please to have opened. She immediately rips open that you offer to her with a large needle (which gives you no more pain than a common scratch), and puts into the vein as much venom as can lie upon the head of her needle, and after binds up the little wound . . . The children or young patients play together all the rest of the day, and are in perfect health to the eighth. Then the fever begins to seize them, and they keep their beds two days, very seldom three. They have very rarely above twenty or thirty in their faces, which never mark; and in eight days' time they are as well as before their illness . . . There is no example of any one that has died in it; and you may believe I am very well satisfied of the safety of the experiment, since I intend to try it on my dear little son.
> (cited by Smith, 1987: 31)

Exclusion from the definition of science of certain domains of learning of particular importance to women and black scientists

The issue of which activities lie within other disciplines, such as technology, is a perennial one. This is especially true for some activities predominantly undertaken by women. Do contributions to cooking and agriculture fall within the compass of science? What about nursing and medicine and the construction of buildings?

Work done by women and black scientists may be unknowable

For various reasons, much of the scientific work done by women has been attributed to men. Even in the twentieth century work done by women has sometimes simply been stolen or unacknowledged (see, for example, the publication by Otto Hahn in his name of Lise Meitner's work on nuclear fission, discussed on p. 85).

Often, though, women's scientific work has gone unacknowledged 'for reasons of propriety'. Many such cases will never be known to us, but some come to light. One instance is the posthumous publications in 1690 of Lady Anne Conway's most important work *The Principles of the Most Ancient and Modern Philosophy, Concerning God, Christ, and the Creature; that is, concerning Spirit, and Matter in General* (originally published in Latin, English translation published in 1692). Anne Conway's name was omitted from the title page and the work attributed to its editor, Francis van Helmost (Alic, 1986). Even in the twentieth century, women sometimes published their scientific work under male pseudonyms. For instance, in 1906 the New York naturalist Anna Botsford published her observations under the name Marian Lee.

Often husbands and brothers fail to acknowledge the contributions made by wives and sisters. One example is Sarah Banks (1744–1818), sister to Joseph Banks, one of the most famous British botanists. It is known that Sarah discussed scientific questions with her brother and acted as his amanuensis, adding her own interpretations as she did so (Ogilvie, 1986). Other instances include: Elizabeth Agassiz (1822–1907), who worked alongside her husband, the biologist Louis Agassiz; Sophia Brahe (1556–1643) who worked with her brother, the astronomer Tycho Brahe; Maria Kirch (1670–1720) who made observations and performed calculations necessary for the publication of her brother's astronomical publications; Amélie Lefrançais de Lalande, the eighteenth century astronomer who assisted her husband, Michel Lefrançais de Lalande, and cousin, Jérôme Lefrançais de Lalande; Nicole-Reine Etable de la Brière Lepaute (1723–1788) who was a distinguished astronomer, almost none of whose work appeared in her name, though much appeared under the names of her husband, Jean André Lepaute, and other collaborators, including Jérôme Lalande and Alexis Claude Clairaut.

Often work done by black people has been appropriated by white people. Martin Bernal (1987) argues that Classical Greek civilization was the result of a mixture of native Europeans and colonizing Africans and Semites rather than a mixture of Indo-European-speaking Hellenes and their indigenous subjects. Hence the title of his book *Black Athena: The Afroasiatic Roots of Classical Civilization*. Bernal argues that the belief that Greek civilization cannot have had Afroasiatic roots is a reflection of racist assumptions that have been especially prevalent in the nineteenth and twentieth centuries.

A related reason why the work of black scientists has often gone unrecognized is that sometimes they were not allowed to patent their discoveries. For instance, in 1858 Jeremiah S. Black [*sic*], Attorney General of the United States of America, ruled that since a patent was a contract between the inventor and the government of the United States, and since a slave was not a citizen of the United States, a slave could not patent anything.

The key to getting one's work appreciated by later generations of historians, is, of course, for one's work to have appeared in some permanent form. Usually this is the written word, though tangible remains such as metal and ceramic artefacts and the fossilized remains of cultivated plants and domesticated animals are important. There are, of course, many cultures throughout the world where desperately little of what once was written survives. What does survive is often still under-researched. The work by Sir Joseph Needham over the last 50 years has transformed our understanding of the contributions to science made in China (see the many volumes in Joseph Needham's *Science and Civilisation in China*, Cambridge University Press). Similar work is currently being undertaken in many other non-Western parts of the world (see van Sertima, 1983; Goonatilake, 1984; Nasr, 1987; Qadir, 1988).

The path to being a scientist, and getting one's work published, is especially difficult unless you are a physically able, white, middle-class male

It is an obvious, but important, point that becoming a scientist and achieving recognition is easier for certain categories of people than for others.

Women have always suffered discrimination in their attempts to get parity of educational and employment opportunity (Fig. 3.1). This has been especially the case for those women wishing to be educated as scientists. The struggle to join the medical profession has been particularly protracted, perhaps because doctors are often well paid and highly esteemed. In the fourth century BCE, the Athenian Agnodike is reported to have disguised herself as a man and studied medicine. At this time many Athenian women were said to die in childhood and from 'private diseases' rather than allow themselves to be seen by a male physician. Agnodike built up a successful and flourishing practice. However, her gender was discovered by the authorities and she was brought to trial for breaking the law – a charge that carried the death penalty. At this, a crowd of protesting women successfully moved the judge to abandon the old law and replace it with one that not only allowed women to practise medicine on their own sex, but provided them with a salary too.

The fourteenth century Italian physician Jacobina Félicie, who worked in France, was prosecuted repeatedly for practising medicine without

Fig. 3.1 Discrimination against women.

a licence. Again, only men were entitled to have licences.

When Elizabeth Garrett Anderson (1836–1917) told her parents she wanted to study medicine her father pronounced the idea 'disgusting' and her mother wept over the coming 'disgrace'. She first underwent a trial period as a surgical nurse at the Middlesex Hospital in London. Although she was supported by the dean, the hospital apothecary and the house physician, the students produced a petition protesting her presence. She wasn't allowed to obtain an MD degree from any British university, so received it in France instead. It took three years of legal battles for the British physician Sophia Jex-Blake (1840–1912) to win the right for women to obtain medical degrees (Ogilvie, 1986).

Of course, such victories have not resulted in the ending of discrimination against women.

A scientific education has always been expensive, so few children from working-class backgrounds ever become famous scientists. One notable exception was Michael Faraday, the nineteenth-century son of a village blacksmith and farm servant, whose scientific achievements are discussed on p. 90. Faraday seems to have owed his academic success to a combination of tremendous determination, exceptional ability and good fortune.

The expense attached to a scientific education is another reason why there are relatively few black scientists. This reason is, of course, compounded by the imposition of Western values on many non-Western countries, and by the removal of tens of millions of black people from their lands during the years of the slave trade.

Disabled people have always found it difficult to obtain employment. Currently the most famous disabled scientist is Stephen Hawking, cosmologist and author of what is perhaps the best-selling scientific book ever – *A Brief History of Time* (Hawking, 1988). Early in 1963, having arrived at Cambridge University in October 1962 to start a PhD, Stephen Hawking was diagnosed as having a rare and incurable disease – amyotrophic lateral sclerosis (generally known as motor neurone disease). It is fair to say that Hawking was fortunate that his research interests lie in theoretical physics. His increasing physical disability was not the handicap that it would have been had he been an empiricist. Indeed, Hawking maintains that one of his crucial insights came into his head precisely because of his disability. One evening in November 1970 Hawking was getting into bed. As he later wrote 'My disability makes this rather a slow process, so I had plenty of time' (Hawking, 1988: 99). It was at this point that Hawking suddenly realized a whole new property of black holes. (Hawking's scientific achievements are discussed on p. 98).

Usually, though, disability, of whatever type, is a hindrance to scientific success. Anne McDonald was 13 when therapist Rosemary Crossley started working at St Nicholas Hospital in Melbourne. Anne has cerebral palsy and doctors had judged her to have a mental age of one. She was force-fed and spent her days lying on the floor. Rosemary Crossley's work showed just how wrong the doctors had been. In Anne's own words:

> I went to St Nicholas Hospital when I was three. The hospital was the state garbage bin where very young children were taken into permanent care . . .
>
> Seeing the occasional television programme gave me some ideas. The Bronowski *Ascent of Man* programmes were critical in bringing me in contact with scientific method . . . When Joey [another child labelled 'profoundly retarded'] taught us about fractions, suddenly everything started to come together. I started doing

> arithmetic for fun. I also tried to work out some constants. I had a go at the speed of light, using the distance of the moon from earth (which had been given coverage during the Apollo missions) . . .
>
> Bronowski covered Pythagoras and I had ample opportunity to think about the implications. The hospital nappies were not square, and every time the nurse had to fold a nappy they had to square it first. I became aware of symmetry and its importance in geometry. To calculate I used a crude abacus based on the clock. I used to work in base twelve. . . .
>
> Sometimes I was hit because I talked with other children, and the nurses thought I was screaming without reason. Since we were always with nurses opportunities for speech were few.
>
> (Baird (1992: 6), based on McDonald and Crossley (1982))

Some of these barriers against women, black people and disabled people, though still highly significant, are weaker now than at most times in the last few hundred years. Ironically, recent achievements and contributions to science by women, black and disabled people may not be covered in schools because their contributions are at too high an intellectual level to be considered appropriate for school teaching. After all, much of science in schools is eighteenth and nineteenth century science. As a corrective I have therefore included in Chapters 6, 7 and 8 some recent scientific contributions by women, black people and disabled people that would otherwise have been omitted.

A critique of the constructivist approach to the teaching of school science

Finally in this chapter, I want to say a little about the constructivist approach to the teaching of school science. It is fair to say that the constructivist approach to science education is by now in a number of countries the paradigm for pupils whatever their ages (Driver, 1983; Osborne and Freyberg, 1985; Needham and Hill, 1987; Scott *et al.*, 1987; Brook *et al.*, 1989; Osborne *et al.*, 1990; Russell and Watt, 1990; Watt and Russell, 1990).

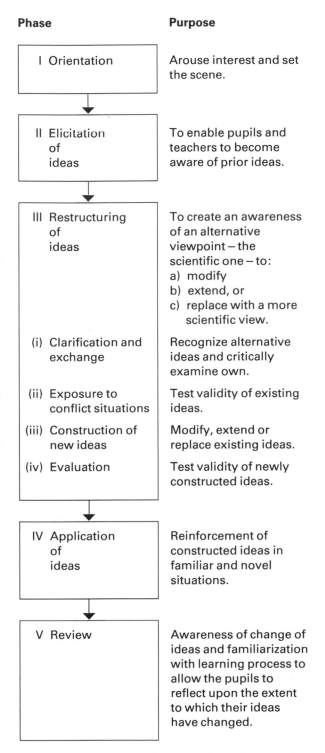

Phase	Purpose
I Orientation	Arouse interest and set the scene.
II Elicitation of ideas	To enable pupils and teachers to become aware of prior ideas.
III Restructuring of ideas	To create an awareness of an alternative viewpoint – the scientific one – to: a) modify b) extend, or c) replace with a more scientific view.
(i) Clarification and exchange	Recognize alternative ideas and critically examine own.
(ii) Exposure to conflict situations	Test validity of existing ideas.
(iii) Construction of new ideas	Modify, extend or replace existing ideas.
(iv) Evaluation	Test validity of newly constructed ideas.
IV Application of ideas	Reinforcement of constructed ideas in familiar and novel situations.
V Review	Awareness of change of ideas and familiarization with learning process to allow the pupils to reflect upon the extent to which their ideas have changed.

Fig. 3.2   The constructivist approach to science teaching.

The constructivist approach to science teaching is summed up in Fig. 3.2.

I am convinced that there is much in a constructivist approach to science education to commend it. I have, however, one concern. There is a real danger that the elicitation of pupils' prior ideas (Phase II in Fig. 3.2) *always* leads to those ideas being replaced. As Fig. 3.2 states, the purpose of Phase III is:

> To create an awareness of an alternative viewpoint – the scientific one – to:
> a) modify
> b) extend, or
> c) replace with a more scientific view.

Similarly, Freyberg and Osborne state:

> As a medical practitioner diagnoses the cause of a symptom before attempting to alleviate it, so the teacher needs to diagnose the viewpoints of her pupils before deciding how to set about modifying them towards more scientifically-acceptable ones.
> (Osborne and Freyberg, 1985: 92)

In other words, the assumption of this approach, at least at present, is that pupils need their ideas to be replaced with more scientific ones. Now, I am not so naive to imagine that all pupils always come to science lessons with valid scientific ideas! But for a teacher to get into a frame of thinking in which the aim is to use the quickest and most effective methods for removing all of certain ways of thinking from children's minds, so that these ways can be replaced with other 'more scientific' ones, does sound rather negating.

I should prefer a frame of thinking in which a teacher started from the assumption that all pupils come to science lessons with ways of thinking *that have so far served them well*. The aim of a science lesson would then be to enable pupils to see *why* their thinking often works, and to allow those pupils who want to to *develop* their thinking, not so much by having it proved wrong to them, but by pursuing it into new areas.

To some, the distinction may seem semantic and immaterial. But I think the attitude of a teacher to their class is likely to differ significantly. To give one example, Osborne and Freyberg (1985) cite the not uncommon occurrence of '17-year-old physics students who, despite the fact that they had learnt and could recall the inverse square law of gravitation, still held to the idea that gravity increased with height above the earth's surface' (Osborne and Freyberg, 1985: 87). Presumably, when such students maintain that gravity increases with height, they are using the word 'gravity' to refer to something akin to what a physicist would term 'gravitational potential energy'. For 'gravity' read 'gravitational potential energy' and every physicist would agree that gravity increases with height above the Earth's surface. Of course, appreciating that this is probably what a 17-year-old means is what every good physics teacher has been doing for decades. The reason science teachers need to know what their pupils and students think is not so that they can better eradicate such thinking, but so that they can use it to enable their pupils and students to move on in their understanding.

The approach I am advocating is more likely to value the variety of ways of thinking that pupils bring to science lessons. After all, as I argued in Chapter 2, there is no single universal scientific way of seeing the world. Indeed often a variety of ways of looking at a scientific problem is a strength: there is no single best way to measure time, purify substances, classify organisms, measure charge, reduce diatomic nitrogen to ammonia, grow plants or magnify objects. As anyone who has ever set a science test or examination knows, half the 'skill' involves choosing situations and writing questions with sufficient precision and care that there will only be a limited number of right answers.

CHAPTER 4

A science department for all

. . . the findings of a number of well conducted surveys are now available. A disconcerting number of these show that there is not a ready link between cognitive learning in science and a positive attitude to science. Indeed, it seems that often the longer students have studied science at school the more their attitude to it declined.

(Fensham, 1988: 20)

In this chapter I will focus on what an individual science department can do to promote effective learning for *all* its pupils/students. By 'science department', I mean those teachers who teach science and the areas in a school where science is taught or science lessons prepared; the term is therefore used to apply both to primary and to secondary schools.

Rather than criticizing large numbers of examples of poor practice, I will try mostly to be more positive, citing good practice, suggesting questions for members of staff in science departments to ask themselves, and providing checklists of recommendations. As far as possible, I will not be doing this separately for ethnic minority pupils, for girls, for working-class pupils, for pupils with special needs, for pupils with physical disabilities, etc. Instead, I will try to provide a unified approach on the grounds that nine times out of ten, what is good science education for one particular segment of the school population is good science education for all (Fig. 4.1).

It might be thought that the ethos and approach of the whole school is so important that the contribution an individual department can make is limited. While it is certainly true that whole school policy is invaluable (Cohen and Cohen, 1986; McLean and Young, 1988; Maitland, 1989; Ainscow, 1991; Gill *et al.*, 1992), research shows that individual departments can make a most signifi-

cant impact. In their book *The School Effect: A Study of Multi-racial Comprehensives*, Smith and Tomlinson (1989) found that there were large significant differences between schools in the examination performance of their pupils at age 16. However, the differences between schools were greater when the results in particular subjects were considered than when the results were considered in total across all subjects. Smith and Tomlinson reached the important conclusion that:

All of these findings can be explained if it is true that the style and content of teaching is determined more at the department level than at the school level.

(Smith and Tomlinson, 1989: 282)

In other words, as every subject teacher knows, individual departments do matter. This is not to suggest that on its own an individual science department can do everything. National, regional and whole-school policies all operate on pupils before they enter a science classroom. Nevertheless, there is much that science departments, and even individual teachers acting within unsympathetic science departments, can achieve.

Staffing issues

It is certainly the case that diversity within the staff of a science department is an asset. Let us make

Fig. 4.1 Gerald, aged 12, investigating a 'babble box' that is part of the 'sound wall' in his classroom. Gerald has no functional vision, in addition to profound learning difficulties. The use of such equipment would enrich the scientific learning of any pupil.

the rather optimistic assumption that outright bias against certain categories of applicant (e.g. black teachers, women returning to teaching after a number of years out of teaching while rearing a family) can be avoided. Often, then, the debate about criteria to be used when making a new appointment centres around whether or not positive discrimination should be applied. A possible way of side-stepping this contentious issue is to shift the focus from the qualifications of the individual applicants for a post to the staffing needs of a department. Just as most senior management teams within a school, particularly if a mixed-sex school, would be unhappy if all its members were male, so a science department whose staff are all of the same sex is less balanced than one where the gender-split is nearer to 50 : 50.

This point applies particularly to secondary schools with a discrete science staff, but essentially the same issue can arise in primary schools. What message is being given if teachers with special responsibility for science are males more often than would be accounted for by chance?

Given the shortage in most countries of girls taking up physical sciences, it is probably particularly unfortunate if the staff of a science department includes few or no women. My anecdotal experience of one Cambridgeshire comprehensive that for a number of years had only female staff in its science department is that I was told by its ex-head of science that the school had the highest proportion of its 16-year-old females going on to study science A levels of any school in the county. More formal evidence comes from Thailand in the mid-1980s (Klainin, 1985; Fensham, 1986). Here 80 per cent of the chemistry teachers and half the physics teachers are women, while both girls and boys study a balanced science course throughout their school careers. Year 10, 11 and 12 girls significantly outscored boys of the same age in six of seven chemistry tests administered to over 700 boys and 700 girls by Sunee Klainin as part of her doctoral study. (There were no gender differences on the seventh test.) In a subsequent study, girls significantly outscored boys on seven of fifteen physics test measures – there being no significant gender differences on the eight other test measures.

Exactly the same point holds about the appointment of black teachers and about teachers from a working-class background. The greater the diversity within the staff of a science department, the more pupils will see particular staff as role models and the easier certain staff will find it to empathize with particular pupils.

Of course, waiting until one's science department makes its next appointment may take time! And, anyway, appointments are not fully in the hands of science departments. I remember one student teacher, having unsuccessfully been interviewed for a job as a science teacher at a school, being told at her de-brief with the head of science that he considered her by far the best applicant but that he had been overruled by a deputy head.

However, other options exist while waiting for new appointments. It may be that responsibilities can be realigned within a department. Are women, black teachers and part-time teachers less likely to be holding key posts? One school I know has for several years successfully job-shared the post of head of science, allowing one of the two people involved twice to go on maternity leave and then return to her post.

How are technicians and classroom assistants used? In secondary schools, science departments are fortunate in that they almost always have more staff attached to them than do other departments. Technicians, in particular, are often the near-exclusive prerogative of science departments. Some technicians would welcome the opportunity to play a more creative role in science education

than merely putting out equipment, clearing it away and doing the washing up. Many science technicians have years of expertise behind them and are more familiar with scientific procedures and the pitfalls of particular investigations than most science staff. Further, as school science technicians are nearly all women, their always being expected to fulfil such a minimalist role reinforces gender stereotypes. A science department for a pluralist society would have a diversity of learning experiences running at any one time. Pupils might sometimes negotiate their equipment needs with a technician. Much the same point holds about specialist staff supporting pupils with disabilities.

Finally, secondary schools still have much to learn from the common practice in primary schools of having volunteer parents in to help with individual reading and other classroom activities. Such help is probably easier to arrange and of more assistance in a science lesson than in most other subjects. I'm not suggesting that every parent should be expected to supervise safety procedures for fractional distillation on their first experience of a science lesson. But science lessons always contain, or should do, groups of pupils working at different speeds on a variety of activities. Volunteer parents, or other adults or older pupils/ students, could be especially helpful for pupils who would benefit from having written information read to them, who welcome assistance with spelling when writing, or who have other particular needs.

Syllabus choice, books and other teaching resources

Countries vary in the extent to which an individual science department or school can choose the science syllabus it wishes to use. If a choice is possible, then similar questions arise as when choosing books, posters or other teaching resources. The questions to ask when selecting syllabuses, books, posters, etc. are:

● What image of science is portrayed? For example, is the topic of motion dominated by

Fig. 4.2 The text by this cartoon in a 1991 publication written for GCSE Science reads: 'Captain Cook exchanged worthless beads and mirrors for gold but then the islanders genuinely thought they were getting a good deal as well; both sides were happy.'

expensive high velocity rockets, thus presenting a Western masculine image of science?

- Are personal, social, economic, technological and ethical aspects dealt with, and if so how?
- Are the applications of science stressed?
- Are scientific principles abstracted from everyday life or are the applications of science merely tagged on at the end of a topic?
- How are men and women and boys and girls portrayed (e.g. always male doctors and female nurses)?
- Are black people and white people shown positively or doing different activities (Fig. 4.2)?
- Are disabled people included, and if so how?
- Would pupils be better off with a few copies of large numbers of different resources than with what is more usually the case – namely multiple sets of just a few resouces?
- Are the resources appropriate for a diversity of pupils needs, interests and abilities?
- Finally, are resources doled out to pupils or can pupils chose which resources (e.g. books, software, videos) to use? Could pupils be involved in choosing which resources are purchased?

The same sorts of questions as these apply to the design and layout of worksheets.

Language issues

The issue of language in science and the boundaries that it can erect are well known (Gardner, 1978, 1980; Cassels and Johnstone, 1980; Bulman, 1985; White and Welford, 1988; Roach *et al.*, 1990; Westley, n.d.). A classic example is provided by *Giky Martables*. The author of this is unknown; the work was retrieved from the floor at a VSO course by Clive Carré of Exeter University:

The following has been taken from a biology text book. The average word knowledge was assessed for 11-year-old pupils. The text was then altered with a nonsense word for all words not in the child's vocabulary. Can you still answer all the questions and get them 'right'?

Giky Martables
It must be admitted, however, that there is an occasional pumtumfence of a diseased condition in wild animals, and we wish to call attention to a remarkable case which seems like a giky martable. Let us return to the retites. In the huge societies of some of them there are guests or pets, which are not merely briscerated but fed and yented, the spintowrow being, in most cases, a talable or spiskant exboration – a sunury to the hosts. The guest or pets are usually small cootles, but sometimes flies, and they have inseresced in a strange hoze of life in the dilesses of the dark ant-hill or peditary – a life of entire dependence on their owners, like that of a petted reekle on its mistress. Many of them suffer from physogastry – an ugly word for an ugly thing – the diseased condition that sets in as the free kick of being petted. In some cases the guest undergoes a perry change. The stoperior body or hemodab becomes tripid in an ugly way and may be prozubered upwards and forwards over the front part of the body, whose size is often bleruced. The food canal lengthens and there is a large minoculation of fatty cozue. The wings fall off. The animals become more or less blind. In short, the animals become generderate and scheformed. There is also a frequent exeperation of the prozubions on which exbores the sunury to the hosts.

(a) What does this remarkable case seem like?
(b) What happens to the guests or pets?
(c) What would you normally expect the spinto-wrow to be like?
(d) How would you recognize a perry change in the guest?
etc., etc.   (Dallas, 1980: 7)

It is all too easy for a teacher's use of oral language to be as intelligible as this piece of prose. Scientific language *does* need at times to be precise and to attach specific meanings either to new words or to words used differently in a non-scientific context. Learning is helped if teachers of science use scientific terminology appropriately. However, scientific language should *aid*, not hinder, understanding. Ideally, knowing the distinctions between the words 'energy', 'power', 'work' and 'force' should be a valuable tool for a pupil, enabling her better to understand the world we live in. Unfortunately, too dogmatic a use of scientific language applied too early in a pupil's school career, or too imprecise a subsequent use of that language by teachers and textbook authors, can discourage or confuse pupils (Jennison and Reiss, 1991). I well remember when I did my teacher training course being told by the lecturer in chemistry education that the word 'fuse' means 'melt' and not anything else. To use it to mean 'join' was wrong. Now as a biologist, I knew he was mistaken – cells do not melt in the process of cell fusion. But even though I *knew* he was wrong, I can still remember feeling really frustrated by this 'expert' telling me how I should speak.

Although science does require a specialist vocabulary, this is still often too large, despite recent attempts to reduce the number of technical terms. If we look at the current (1989) edition of the UK Institute of Biology's booklet *Biological Nomenclature: Recommendations on Terms, Units and Symbols*, we find that the following words and terms are amongst those considered appropriate for use by 13–16-year-olds: 'amnion', 'amphetamine', 'anabolism', 'analgesic', 'anticoagulant', 'articulation' and 'autotroph', to name just some of the 61 words and terms beginning with the letter 'a'. I find it difficult to believe that all of these are really necessary.

The list for 16–18-year-olds is even more daunting. There are 156 words or terms listed that begin with the letter 'a'. (I should like to know how many French words beginning with the letter 'a' the typical 16–18-year-old studying French knows. I have a horrible feeling a science student may be expected to learn more specialist vocabulary than a linguist.) Amongst these 156 are the following: 'acromegaly', 'adenylate cyclase', 'agglutinogen'. 'aldosterone', 'ampulla', 'androecium', 'anisogamy', 'antherozoid', 'antipodal cell', 'appeasement display', 'archenteron', 'areolar connective tissue', 'ascospore' and 'association centre'. Unless you teach biology to 16–18-year-olds in England or Wales, I shouldn't think there's the faintest chance that you have heard, let alone know the meaning, of all of these.

Of course, science doesn't just have a specialized vocabulary; it often demands a very precise use of familiar words and of grammar and syntax: 'power is the *rate of doing* work', 'producers *support* carnivores', 'an atom is the *smallest part* of an element *which can ever exist*', '*in the ratio of*', '*whereas*', '*consequently*', '*subsequently*', '*simultaneously*', '*previously*', '*consecutive*', etc., not to mention words that have more than one meaning, for example, 'since', 'as' and 'for'. It is more difficult for a teacher to realize how such use of language is unfamiliar to many pupils than it is to appreciate that the first time one mentions 'chlorophyll', for instance, the word needs to be explained and written for pupils to see (see Gardner, 1978, 1980).

Suggestions to do with language issues

It must be emphasized that very few of these suggestions are meant solely for pupils being taught in a language that is not their home language. Although such pupils are likely to benefit from these suggestions, so will almost all pupils. Similarly, some of the suggestions that are particularly appropriate for pupils with certain physical disabilities (e.g. poor eyesight, hardness of hearing) will benefit many other pupils. As is usually the case in teaching, approaches that work well for particular groups of pupils generally work well for most pupils.

- Remember that there are four relatively distinct language skills – listening, speaking, reading and writing. Pupils need practice with, and teaching in, each of these.
- Talk and write in short sentences.
- Don't use two words where one will do; avoid unnecessary polysyllabic words.
- Take care with handwriting (on blackboards, whiteboards, OHP transparencies and work-sheets and when marking/correcting pupils' work).
- Explain all specialized use of vocabulary, not just technical terms.
- When helpful, explain the origins of specialized terms (e.g. 'photosynthesis', 'electromagnetic spectrum') and provide mnemonics and other memory aids (e.g. *sugar* = *su*crose; 'red' is a shorter word than 'blue' and 'acid' is a shorter word than 'alkali').
- Write down specialized vocabulary and/or encourage pupils to keep a vocabulary book.
- Consider using boxes, arrows and standard logos (e.g. a drawing of a pair of safety goggles) instead of only written verbal instructions to guide pupils.
- Encourage pupils to talk about science with their peers in the language and terms they want (whether or not they are bilingual).
- Be careful if using metaphors or similes and introduce them and explain them as such.
- Label shelves and cupboards where equipment is kept in the language(s) familiar to pupils. (I have not managed to find a commercial organization that does this. One possibility is that such labelling could be done by pupils themselves.)
- Provide a copy of the Laboratory Rules in each pupil's home language (e.g. Fig. 4.3).
- Ensure that all writing intended for pupils is sufficiently large and clear to be visible – enlarging photocopiers can work wonders providing the original is of sufficient quality.
- Ensure that all relevant oral contributions, whether by the teacher or other pupils, are audible.
- Consider enabling pupils to record their work using word processors or on video or audio tapes (Fig. 4.4).

ਪ੍ਰਯੋਗਸ਼ਾਲਾ (ਲੈਬਾਰਟਰੀ) ਦੇ ਨਿਯਮ PUNJABI

੧. ਕਿਸੇ ਵਿਦਿਆਰਥੀ ਨੂੰ ਬਿਨਾਂ ਪੁੱਛੇ ਪਰਯੋਗਸ਼ਾਲਾ ਦੇ ਅੰਦਰ ਆਣ ਦੀ ਇਜਾਜ਼ਤ ਨਹੀਂ ਹੈ।

੨. ਪ੍ਰਯੋਗਸ਼ਾਲਾ ਵਿਚ ਕਦੀ ਨਾ ਦੌੜੇ ਜਾਂ ਕਾਹਲ ਨਾਲ ਏਧਰ ਓਧਰ ਚੱਲੇ।

੩. ਅਪਣੇ ਕੋਟ ਜਾਂ ਬਸਤੇ ਮੇਜ਼ਾਂ ਉੱਤੇ ਕਦੀ ਨਾ ਰੱਖੇ।

੪. ਲੰਮੇ ਵਾਲਾਂ ਨੂੰ ਜਾਂ ਖੁੱਲੇ ਕਪੜਿਆਂ ਨੂੰ ਪਿੱਛੇ ਬਨ੍ਹ ਲਵੇ।

੫. ਅਧਿਆਪਕ ਦੇ ਕਹਿਣ ਤੇ ਅਪਣੀ ਹਿਫ਼ਾਜ਼ਤ ਲਈ ਚਸ਼ਮਾ ਜ਼ਰੂਰ ਪਹਿਣ ਲਵੇ।

੬. ਗੈਸ, ਪਾਣੀ ਤੇ ਬਿਜਲੀ ਦੀਆਂ ਚੀਜ਼ਾਂ ਨਾਲ ਕਦੇ ਕੋਈ ਛੇੜਖਾਨੀ ਨਾ ਕਰੇ।

੭. ਜੇ ਕੋਈ ਦੁਰਘਟਨਾ ਹੋ ਜਾਏ ਜਾਂ ਕੋਈ ਚੀਜ਼ ਟੁੱਟ ਜਾਏ ਤਾਂ ਤੁਰੰਤ ਅਧਿਆਪਕ ਨੂੰ ਖਬਰ ਕਰ ਦਿਉ।

੮. ਬਿਨਾਂ ਪੁੱਛੇ ਕਦੀ ਕਿਸੇ ਚੀਜ਼ ਨੂੰ ਚੱਖ ਕੇ ਨਾ ਦੇਖੇ।

੯. ਜੇ ਹੱਥਾਂ ਜਾਂ ਕਪੜਿਆਂ ਤੇ ਕੋਈ ਚੀਜ਼ ਡੁੱਲ੍ਹ ਜਾਏ ਤਾਂ ਓਸੇ ਵੇਲੇ ਧੋ ਲਵੇ।

੧੦. ਕੋਈ ਟੈਸ ਟਿਊਬ ਕੂੜਾ, ਟੁਟਿਆ ਕੱਚ, ਕਾਗਜ਼ ਜਾਂ ਲਕੜੀ ਦੀ ਛਿੱਲਤਰ ਕਦੇ ਸਿੰਕ ਵਿਚ ਨਾ ਸੁੱਟੇ; ਇਹਨਾਂ ਨੂੰ ਕੂੜੇ ਦੇ ਡੱਬੇ ਵਿਚ ਸੁੱਟੇ।

੧੧. ਪ੍ਰਯੋਗਸ਼ਾਲਾ ਤੋਂ ਬਿਨਾਂ ਪੁੱਛੇ ਕਦੀ ਵੀ ਕੋਈ ਚੀਜ਼ ਲੈ ਕੇ ਬਾਹਰ ਨਾ ਜਾਓ।

੧੨. ਅਧਿਆਪਕ ਦੀ ਦਿੱਤੀਆਂ ਹਿਦਾਇਤਾਂ ਨੂੰ ਬੜੇ ਧਿਆਨ ਨਾਲ ਸੁਣੇ ਤੇ ਠੀਕ ਉਹੀ ਕਰੇ ਜੋ ਤੁਹਾਨੂੰ ਆਖਿਆ ਗਿਆ ਹੈ।

Fig. 4.3 School science laboratory safety rules in Punjabi.

- Strike a balance between requiring pupils always to report their work in a formal mode traditionally considered appropriate for science ('A sample of calcium carbonate was obtained . . .') and never enabling pupils to realize that science does have a distinctive language which needs to be communicated intelligibly with precision ('My frend she give me the white rock . . .').
- Consider whether to require pupils to play little language games. For example, provide numbered instructions for an experiment in the wrong order, so that the pupils have to put them in the right order before beginning the practical. The appropriateness of such activities depends

Fig. 4.4 Bengali student working at a computer in a science lesson at a secondary school in Birmingham.

on the age and nature of the pupils. At best, such an approach can be enjoyed by pupils and promote valuable scientific discussion and learning. At worst, the activity is perceived either as patronising or even deceitful – 'teacher trying to trip us up'.

- When setting reading tasks, ensure that what is being read is appropriate to the pupil. Where possible, get pupils to engage with the text in some way. Usually this is done by getting pupils to answer questions on the text. Other approaches include getting pupils to translate from one mode of communication into another (e.g. prose into diagrams) and to rewrite for a different audience (e.g. a passage on decomposition could be rewritten as if by a garden centre providing instructions on how to make compost).

- Keep alert to the possibility that some pupils would benefit from specialist equipment (e.g. glasses, hearing aids, Braille transcripts, pocket tape recorders).

- Liaise well in advance of lessons, even if only very briefly, with language and other classroom assistants.

Teaching strategies

It isn't, of course, possible to cover the whole field of teaching strategies appropriate for science teaching in a few pages (see, in particular, Newton, 1988; White, 1988; Bentley and Watts, 1989; Woolnough, 1991). But I can emphasize certain teaching strategies that may be particularly appropriate for a science education for a pluralist society. After looking at practical work (done in almost all science teaching) and role play (done rarely in science teaching), I consider what all this might mean for one particular scientific activity that doesn't easily fall into Chapters 6 to 8, namely 'measurement'.

Practical work

Practical work is done in school science lessons for a variety of reasons. All too often, though, what is done, or how it is valued by teachers, is biased towards certain groups. Murphy (1991) reviews the research evidence on how girls and boys behave differently when doing practical work. On average (and to any such generalizations there are always many significant exceptions) girls interact with teachers differently. Many of their contacts include requests for help about what to do next. Too often teachers may accept girls' dependence on them, tell them what to do and thus reinforce feelings of relative helplessness. The problem is exacerbated by the extra time teachers often spend with boys trying to ensure that they don't misbehave or get injured or damage equipment. As she concludes 'The combination of girls' timidity and boys' bravado lead to girls being marginalised in laboratories' (Murphy, 1991: 118–19).

When arranging practical work for pupils with special educational needs, including pupils with severe learning difficulties, it often helps to break down practical activities in small steps. At the same time, consider how apparatus or other facilities in a laboratory can be modified to provide the maximum opportunity for relevant practical work (e.g. Fig. 4.5). Excellent suggestions and case studies are contained in Fagg *et al.* (1990), Jones and Butcher (1990), Best (1992), Jones and Purnell (1992a,b) and NCC (1992a,b,c).

Whenever possible, make practical investigations open-ended. This helps pupils to own what they are doing, to work at their own pace and to involve themselves in their work. Project work can be especially valuable, as it requires pupils to be scientists. Similarly, problem-solving is effective, provided every lesson doesn't become 'Today we are going to design a . . .'. A good lesson plan is like a fine tune: sufficient predictability to comfort the listener; enough variety to engage her attention.

Finally, an attractive laboratory can work wonders. Get some plants and a couple of aquaria. Have some displays of pupils' work – not just posters and practical write-ups but on-going projects in all the areas of science. If you're worried all this will take too long, see if a pupil will volunteer to water the plants and feed the fish, at least during term time. If ugly, damaged, old-fashioned goggles and lab coats are putting some pupils off science, replace them with new ones and only insist on their use when it's necessary. And don't give the impression that all science is dangerous. Be positive and precise when giving safety instructions. For instance, stress the correct way to adjust the flame of a Bunsen burner or heat a test tube containing liquids.

Role play/discussion of personal, social and political issues

Role plays can be a most effective way of encouraging empathy and enabling pupils to see others' points of view. Many pupils enjoy writing and acting out scripts or character descriptions – though undue stereotyping needs to be guarded against. Here are two examples: one real, the other fictitious but based on genuine data. In each case there are various ways of using the material. At one extreme would be a full-scale role play involving large numbers of pupils each playing different roles. At the other extreme, pupils could individually write down their reactions to the pieces. Between these two extremes there is obviously a variety of other pedagogical approaches. I imagine many science teachers would favour small group discussions followed by some kind of plenary discussion. If role play is used, it is most important that at the end of the exercise pupils derole, in other words that they are quite clear that they are no longer in role, but have returned to their own life. English/drama teachers can, if necessary, advise on the various ways of ensuring deroling takes place.

Fig. 4.5 Madeleine, aged 12, in a science lesson at Impington Village College, Cambridgeshire. Madeleine has cerebral palsy. She is using a communication board to help her communicate with a classmate while they are doing a practical together.

Example 1: Real

This piece could be used when teaching about sickle cell anaemia and could introduce the question of whether sufficient medical and research funds are devoted to sickle cell disease which almost exclusively attacks black people.

I had just ridden into town on my bike. It was quite cold and on my return my teeth were on edge. Like I'd just eaten an ice cream. Three hours later, the pain was getting quite bad. It settled for a while and then the pain went to my back. Now my back and jaw were both hurting. So my friends decided that it was Casualty time. I followed reluctantly. Once in Casualty, things went from bad to unbearable very fast. I always reached Casualty at all hospitals with a mixed feeling of relief and dread. On this occasion I had good reason to feel dread. I

didn't see a doctor for another one and a half hours. He quickly looked me over and then stalked out mumbling something about haemotologists and their responsibility. Two hours later I was still waiting. I was trying desperately to stop myself from crying out loud. I didn't want to break down in front of my friends. However, I couldn't help it and I started to bawl like a baby. My friends had asked what the hold-up was on two occasions and at one point I had fallen off the trolley. I got up, saying that I had had enough. I went and asked: 'How much longer?' between sobs. I was calmly told that: 'Doctor was on his way.' My jaw had clamped shut with the pain by this time. After a four and half hour wait, I was finally admitted to the ward and given pethidine [a pain-killer].

Once on the ward, I was constantly being told off for all the noise that I was making. I felt guilty enough without being told; I didn't want to keep everyone awake. After about two hours I was moved to another bay to keep some other patients awake. By morning I had a temperature of 39.5 and I was delirious. Nothing else existed except the agony I was experiencing. When the doctors came, they asked stupid questions like, how bad was the pain? Christ, how I hated that question, and they all ask it, never fail. Pain is pain, never mind what kind. They all hurt. How in God's name do you describe the kind of pain that you are experiencing?

I was only a patient for six days. It felt like six months.

Sickle Cell Society (n.d.: 67–8)

Example 2: Fictitious

This piece could be used when teaching about water, energy or the conservation of forests.

Franca stood up and stretched. She felt tired. She had got up at five o'clock in the morning and by now it was four o'clock in the afternoon. Time to go home. It was the sowing season. Franca and the other women had spent about eight hours that day sowing manioc, a very important food plant in Zaire.

Now it was time to stop sowing and start collecting firewood. About 30–40 kg of firewood would have to be collected for the preparation of the evening meal. Nowadays collecting firewood seemed to take Franca and the other women longer than it used to. Franca preferred collecting the water. At least then she could walk to the well with her friends, even if it did take a long time. Her family of seven would need about 40–50 litres of water daily. Franca could carry about 10–15 litres on her head at a time, so she would have to make four trips to the well. The well was two kilometres from her home.

The topic of measurement

For some rather sad reason, school science lessons rarely celebrate the tremendous richness with which humans have measured, and still do measure, such variables as length, mass, volume and temperature. Instead, exactly the opposite happens. Pupils are told that traditional ways of measuring things are 'not good enough' or 'less scientific' than what they will now have to learn instead. What happens, then, is that many schools rarely use units such as inches, feet, acres, gallons or degrees Fahrenheit – or if they do, they do so rather guiltily, implying that 'we really should be using litres, but we'll just do this in pints because pints are easier, aren't they, and science is difficult and all a bit strange, isn't it?'.

This is all very regrettable. Language experts, whether academic linguists or school language teachers, don't spend all their time trying to reduce the number of languages that people speak – or at least, they shouldn't, though I realize that the educational systems of almost all countries effectively rank languages in terms of their acceptability. In England and Wales, for example, we get English first, Welsh second or last depending on how far west you are, French second, German and Spanish third, Italian and Russian fourth, Urdu, Gujarati, Bengali and Punjabi fifth and most other languages and dialects (e.g. Turkish, Creole) pretty well nowhere. By and large, though, language experts are usually concerned to *increase* the number of languages spoken.

So why do science educators and the people who set examinations and other assessment tasks in science feel they have to get everyone to use the Système International d'Unités? This seems particularly ironic, as my experience is that most professional scientists are actually the last people to insist on standardization, being perfectly able to use, for example, both the Fahrenheit and the Centigrade scale of temperature measurement as well, of course, as using degrees Kelvin when appropriate.

Much good science teaching would result if pupils, both in the primary and the secondary age range, were explicitly taught about the *diversity* of approaches used in measurement. Amongst the units and scales which pupils could research to discover their origins and their advantages and disadvantages are the following:

inch	ton
foot	kilogramme
yard	tonne
mile/nautical mile	second
metre	minute

light-year	hour
acre	day
grain	week
carat	month
Avoirdupois ounce	year
fluid ounce	degrees Fahrenheit
Troy ounce	degrees Celsius
pound	degrees Kelvin
stone	Beaufort scale
	Richter scale

There is some useful information about some of these in Whitrow (1988) and Bridgeman (n.d.) and see p. 95, but good encyclopaedias and reference books are often best. In addition, of course, pupils may find out a great deal about units and scales by asking older family members how they used to, or still do, measure things.

Other science department issues

Arrangement of pupils in classrooms

I am not going here to look at the arguments for and against single-sex schools, nor at whether or not pupils with severe learning difficulties should be integrated into the rest of the school system or segregated. Neither of these questions can be answered by a science department on its own. However, a science department could, just about, decide to provide separate classes for girls and boys. The limited amount of data, much of which relate to mathematics, suggest that providing separate mathematics and science classes for girls and boys can sometimes significantly increase the educational attainment of girls (Samuel, 1983a; Deem, 1984; Dayton, 1992).

For the great majority of science departments, which will no doubt continue to teach boys and girls together, the first priority is to ensure that boys don't hog all the places at the front. In Thailand, where girls do better in chemistry than boys (p. 42), Klainin (1985) observed twelve co-educational classrooms and found that, in general, the girls sat in the front half of the class and, if anything, were more dominant in oral inter-actions. Good practice relating to girls applies to other groups of pupils, with appropriate changes of emphasis. Don't, for example, allow pupils from middle-class backgrounds to dominate the seats in the centre and at the front of the classroom at the expense of pupils from working-class backgrounds.

The best time to ensure that a seating pattern is as a teacher wants it, is the first time a group comes into a classroom. Attempting to change well-established seating arrangements can produce negative results. I have seen teachers disrupt long-standing friendship groups, which can back-fire. One teacher I know insists that each table has both girls and boys and black and white pupils represented on it. As each table only seats four or five pupils, this requires a lot of rearranging! However, without going so far, it is still possible to ensure that different groupings of pupils are spread fairly evenly around the classroom.

Challenging racist, sexist and other discriminatory behaviour

There really should be a whole-school policy on this and it should be followed. Any teacher, ideally any adult on school premises, should make it clear to the perpetrator of the discrimination, the person/people discriminated against and any onlookers/those in earshot at the time of the discrimination that such behaviour is completely unacceptable. In addition, any offending literature should be confiscated and graffiti quickly removed. If these procedures are adopted, and if a school has appropriate sanctions in place, discriminatory behaviour on school premises should be greatly reduced. All this may, however, do little to alter underlying prejudicial attitudes. Good sex education and good tutorial work can help reduce sexism, racism and other sorts of discrimination, for example against pupils with disabilities. It is possible that science education could play a contributory role in enabling pupils scientifically to examine whether such discrimination is reasonable (see 'Teaching about race' on pp. 60–61).

Assessment issues

It is probably impossible to come up with a single assessment instrument that is universally fair to all pupils. For example, gender bias would be accentuated by having science tests that were either all essays or all multiple choice. Given this, the best procedure is probably to adopt a range of assessment procedures.

A more subtle problem is that valid contributions may not always be recognized. Murphy (1991) gives an example where pupils aged 8 to 15 were given the task of designing boats to go round the world:

> The pupils' designs covered a wide range but there were striking differences between those of boys and girls. The majority of the boats designed by primary or lower secondary school boys were powerboats or battleships of some kind or other. The detail the boys included varied but generally there was elaborate weaponry and next to no living facilities. Other features included detailed mechanisms for movement, navigation and waste disposal. The girls' boats were generally cruisers with a total absence of weaponry and a great deal about living quarters and requirements, including food supplies and cleaning materials (notably absent from the boys' designs). Very few of the girls' designs included any mechanistic detail.
>
> (Murphy, 1991: 120)

It is clear that if a teacher had in mind that what was crucial was the mechanical ability to go round the world, then the girls' designs would do less well. Related to this is the Pygmalian effect, i.e. teachers tend to give work higher marks if it is from pupils whom they expect to get high marks. Experiments have shown that science scripts with boys' names on them are frequently marked significantly higher than identical scripts with girls' names on them (Spear, 1984). The use of objective, criterion-referenced marking can *help* alleviate this problem, but will not necessarily overcome it, as no valid marking procedure can be totally reliable.

A possible way out of the difficulty of deciding whether or not a teacher's assessment procedure is biased against certain pupils, is to allow a significant input from self- and peer-assessment. This allows each pupil to make clear the frame of reference in which they were operating. I know that records of achievement and profiles can take up a lot of time, but once it is accepted that a pupil's point of view has real validity and that no single teacher's assessment scheme can be equally appropriate for all pupils, then the arguments in favour of them become very strong.

Staff INSET and compiling a department policy

I have left till last in this chapter what many will consider should come first. Department policies can be valuable in focusing thoughts, helping to reinforce existing good practice and enabling change. However, despite good intentions, they can end up taking a great deal of time and effort, and may divide departments into progressives and conservatives. Perhaps it is sufficient to say that they can be beneficial but need not be assumed to be essential. Sometimes ethos is sufficient. Much the same can be said about INSET. At best, it can be a way of a science department choosing what it wants to do with some of a school's INSET budget and then putting such choices into practice. At worst it can become 'another set of meetings'. There are some excellent suggestions for INSET appropriate to science education for a pluralist society in Hollins (1986), Pugh (1990), Thorp (1991) and NCC (1992b).

CHAPTER 5

Teaching controversial issues in science

In the past few years I [Julian Brown, Science Unit, BBC] have heard a lot of loose talk about how, thanks to modern physics, science and religion no longer clash. So much that they are now reputed to be living together in peaceful, blissful harmony. Hogwash! I cannot think of a time when the evidence against religious belief has been so damning.

(Brown, 1991: 46)

In this chapter I start by defining what is meant by a 'controversial issue' and examine different ways in which a teacher might attempt to teach about controversial issues. I then go on to consider some specific examples of controversial issues in science teaching and look at how they might be tackled.

Teaching controversial issues in general

An appropriate definition of a controversial issue is provided by Dearden:

> A matter is controversial if contrary views can be held on it without those views being contrary to reason.

(Dearden, 1984: 86)

The crucial phrase here is 'without those views being contrary to reason'. Although there are times when it is a matter of controversy as to whether or not an issue is controversial, I suspect that most science teachers would regard each of the following statements as controversial:

- The evidence for evolution disproves the creation accounts found in most religions.
- *Homo sapiens* can be classified into a number of different races.
- Nuclear power is an effective way of reducing the magnitude of the greenhouse effect as it doesn't result in the production of carbon dioxide.

It is my contention that science education ought to tackle such matters. Below I will defend this statement and try to provide some guidance as to how science teachers might enable their pupils/students to learn about such issues appropriately. Before doing that, though, it may help to consider three different approaches to the teaching of a controversial issue, whether in science or elsewhere (Bridges, 1986).

First, the approach of *advocacy*. Here the teacher argues for the position she/he holds. For example, one teacher might argue in favour of the view 'There is conflict between scientific and religious views about the origin of the world'; another, from a different standpoint, might argue in favour of the assertion 'Evolutionary theories about the origin of species do not disprove the validity of religious faith'. The position of advocacy is intellectually tenable but runs into the problem that in a classroom a teacher is, of course, almost always in a more powerful position than any of her/his students. There is therefore a danger that when a teacher adopts a model of advocacy in the teaching of a controversial issue, she or he may end up trampling on a student's autonomy.

A second approach is one of *affirmative neutrality*. This is a type of teaching in which the teacher presents to her/his students as many sides of a controversy as possible, without, at least initially, indicating which she/he personally supports. This approach obviously has the advantage of being more balanced than the approach of advocacy, though, by its very nature, a controversial issue is one for which a teacher may find it particularly difficult to give a balanced presentation. Indeed, precisely what would constitute a balanced presentation is, for many issues, itself controversial. A further difficulty with this approach is that the lesson may end up being very didactic and fail to engage the interest and involvement of many in a class.

A third approach is one of *procedural neutrality*. Here the teacher acts as a facilitator. Information about the controversy and different points of view are elicited from pupils and available in the form of resource material. The teacher does not reveal her/his own position. This last approach has many advantages. However, the compilation of suitable resource material does require a considerable input of time by the teacher. Without these appropriate resources, the approach runs the risk of failing to elicit a sufficient range of views from the students, in which case the lesson may become unbalanced or require the teacher to intervene in a manner more appropriate to the approaches of affirmative neutrality or even advocacy.

Teaching the relationship between science and religion

The ever present issue of the relationship between science and religion has been brought into closer prominence in English and Welsh schools within the last few years by the publication in England and Wales of the National Curriculum in Science. In the latest version of the Science National Curriculum we read in the General Introduction to the Programme of study for both Double Science and Single Science at Key Stage 4 (for 14–16-year-olds):

> *The nature of scientific ideas*: pupils should be given opportunities to develop their knowledge and understanding of how scientific ideas change through time and how their nature and the use to which they are put are affected by the social, moral, spiritual and cultural contexts in which they are developed. In doing so they should begin to

recognise that, while science is an important way of thinking about experience, it is not the only way.

(DES and Welsh Office, 1991: 22)

There have been a variety of responses to the question of how science teachers should tackle what is often referred to as 'the science/religion issue'. For example, at one pole, Michael Poole maintains that beliefs and values are inherent in the nature of science, and argues for a Christian input to the discussion (Poole, 1990a, b). Brian Woolnough has argued against the segregation of science and religion in the classroom and the exclusion of religion from science lessons (Woolnough, 1989). At the other pole, Colin Siddons and Bernard Spurgin maintain that:

> . . . the beliefs conjectured by scientists, as scientists, are held subject to refutation. There can be no justification, therefore, for discussing beliefs in science and beliefs in religion as if they belong to the same class. Let teachers of religion tackle supposed conflicts between religion and science if they wish to do so and are well enough informed to do so competently . . . Science teachers have more than enough to do . . . They should not allow themselves to be seduced into taking heed of the desires of non-scientists to adulterate science syllabuses with non-science.
>
> (Siddons and Spurgin, 1990: 146)

Similarly, Martin Monk (1990) accuses Michael Poole of failing to take an academic stance towards his topic and instead producing a partisan tract.

All this suggests that the relationship between science and religion is controversial. However, this does not mean, of course, that everyone sees the science/religion issue as controversial. For example, many atheists and theists, in their separate ways, see the issue as relatively uncontroversial. For an atheist, science and religion are often simply seen to be in conflict; for a theist, science and religion are often seen to complement or reinforce each other. A matter is controversial not if everyone agrees it is controversial, but if differing views on the subject can validly be held.

Let us take it, then, that the relationship

between science and religion is controversial. This does not, though, necessarily mean that it ought to be tackled by science teachers. It is necessary therefore, to ask: 'Should science teachers deal in science lessons with the relationship between science and religion?'.

Should science teachers deal in science lessons with the relationship between science and religion?

I can imagine a number of reasons why many science teachers might answer 'No' to this question. One possible reason is: 'I'm not sure this issue ought to be raised in science lessons.' Perhaps I don't believe the issue arises at all – I might feel that science and religion don't interact. This might be because I can't accept the validity of any religious suppositions or because I feel that science and religion occupy distinctive spheres of knowledge which, by virtue of their distinctiveness, fail to interact. Another reason for answering 'I'm not sure this issue ought to be raised in science lessons' is that although I accept that science and religion do interact, I don't feel this interaction should be tackled in science lessons. Perhaps it shouldn't be tackled at school at all, or if it is to be tackled in school, it should be done in RE or PSE or general studies time.

A second reason why someone might answer 'No' to this question is: 'I haven't been trained to deal with this issue as a science teacher.' Here the person may feel that the issue should be addressed in science lessons but doesn't feel competent or confident about doing it herself or himself. I suppose this is a bit like the reason why many primary schools, until recently, did little physics. It wasn't that on principle thousands of primary teachers objected to the teaching of friction or density or whatever; it was just that primary teachers hadn't ever been adequately trained to deal with these topics.

A third reason for answering 'No' centres around: 'My own beliefs are personal to me.' (Here I am using 'belief' in the widest possible sense; for some people agnosticism or atheism can

be described as a belief.) In this instance the feeling is that the privacy of the teacher might be invaded if she or he started discussing issues of science/religion. This is similar to what some teachers feel about sex education. They would rather not deal with aspects of sex education that involve talking about one's own beliefs, values and behaviour.

A fourth reason is related to the third, but focuses on the possible consequences of dealing with science/religion to the pupils or students in one's class. Here the reason is: 'I don't want to influence my pupils/students in matters of personal belief.' In this instance the concern is that allowing a discussion of science/religion issues might indoctrinate members of the class (either for or against religion).

These reasons seem to me to carry a great deal of weight. Although I feel that the answer to the question I posed is 'Yes', in other words that science teachers should deal in science lessons with the relationship between science and religion, I can see only one fundamental argument to support this assertion. This is: 'The issue is important for an understanding of what science is and how it proceeds.' In other words, there is a *scientific* rationale for science teachers dealing with the relationship between science and religion. My own view is that unless there is this scientific reason for dealing with science/religion issues, there is no reason why science teachers should have to deal with the matter.

The strongest argument as to why science teachers should deal with the relationship between science and religion in school science lessons is that it is good science so to do. That is, science teachers need to enable their pupils or students to consider explicitly the domain of science, the procedures by which scientific knowledge accumulates and the ways in which this knowledge differs in methodology and scope from religious, aesthetic and psychological knowledge. In this way students should emerge from schools with a better understanding of what science is and how it proceeds. They will also then be in a better position to assess for themselves the various claims made about the relationship between science and religion.

Guidelines for dealing with the relationship between science and religion

Before going any further, I want to argue in favour of the following proposition: 'Guidelines on this issue should be applicable to any science teacher whatever the nature of her/his religious beliefs.' For some this may seem a surprising or unrealistic aim. However, I put it forward for two reasons. First, I think it a morally defensible principle. I don't like the idea of producing guidelines that could only apply to atheists or to Jews or whoever. It seems better to provide, if it is possible, guidelines that can be agreed to by all science teachers. Secondly, as well as this aim being, I feel, morally the most defensible, I think it wise in the sense that guidelines which, for instance, are only likely to be followed by those of a Christian persuasion, may cause unhelpful divisions within science departments.

So the aim, therefore, will be to produce guidelines with which, to give some specific categories of people, an atheist, a Muslim, a liberal Christian or a fundamentalist of any religion can agree. I will first look at when such teaching should be done, and then give one example of how it might be done.

I can see three main strategies as to when a science teacher might tackle the relationship of science and religion.

1 First, and I admit this has often been my practice, the teacher simply waits until the science/religion issue comes up before dealing with it. An advantage of this approach is that you don't have to go to the trouble of preparing any resources and you reduce the risk of being accused of indoctrination – because you wait until a pupil brings the issue up.
2 Secondly, a teacher can explicitly raise the science/religion issue when dealing with certain key scientific topics, such as evolution or cosmology. This allows one to be better prepared, but may run the risk of implicitly condoning a conflict model of science and religion, in which a few key scientific areas become battlegrounds.
3 A third approach is explicitly to raise the science/religion issue when dealing with the status of scientific knowledge. For some classes this approach may be too abstract. However, it does avoid the debate focusing on just a couple of *causes célèbres*, and allows for a fuller discussion about the nature of scientific knowledge.

As to how such teaching might be done, my own experience, having tried the three approaches outlined above of advocacy, affirmative neutrality and procedural neutrality, is that I feel most comfortable starting from a position of procedural neutrality. I follow this with a discussion which might result in my adopting the approaches of affirmative neutrality or even advocacy; this would depend on the range and balance of comments elicited from the group with which I am working.

I have tried the approach of procedural neutrality with some success with students in initial teacher training. Without revealing my own views about the Darwin–Wallace theory of natural selection and its implications for theology and religious faith, I provided students with a wide range of materials detailing how Darwin's *On The Origin of Species By Means of Natural Selection* was received after its publication on 24 November 1859. They were also given background information about life in Europe at the time. The students then divided themselves into four groups and desk-top published the front page of a newspaper of that time reacting to Darwin's book.

One group produced *The Times*, which, though it discussed the book, gave pride of place to Garibaldi's campaigns in Italy. Another group produced *Nature*, which, though generally positive about the book, stressed the controversy caused in the scientific establishment. A third group produced *The Church Times* which gave pride of place to Lord Wilberforce's scientific assessment of Darwin's theory. Finally, the fourth group formed a feminist workers' co-operative and produced a tabloid called *The Splurge*. Their lead story was that 'All Men are Apes. Its Official!!!'.

Other teaching approaches

Within the framework of procedural neutrality as defined by Bridges (1986), the desk-top publishing approach outlined above allowed students to engage with the relevant issues in a constructive manner (constructive in the literal sense that they were able to make and remake their thinking). A range of possible teaching strategies appropriate for science education for a pluralist society was considered in Chapter 4. Here, though, before going on to suggest what might be a teacher's aims when teaching certain specific controversial issues in science, it is worth stressing that there are four essentials that a teacher must provide when allowing pupils to wrestle with a controversial matter:

1 A classroom where pupils can appreciate the points of view held by others – that is, empathize with others.
2 An environment in which pupils can safely experiment with their own thoughts about the matter being considered.
3 Appropriate boundaries to indicate what, if any, are unacceptable behaviours.
4 A systematic exposure to the issues at stake and a sufficiently balanced consideration of the range of views held.

As the third of these may sound draconian and inappropriate for a liberal education, let me clarify. Most teachers would not allow a range of pupil behaviours, such as being rude, interrupting and shouting, not to mention hitting another pupil. Further, I disagree with Wellington (1986) who maintains that:

> All viewpoints should be expressed in the discussion (even if they are not held by all participants) with equal force and fairness, and should be given equal time and space.
>
> (Wellington, 1986: 152)

Although such a procedure appears very balanced and reasonable, a teacher might decide that, however calmly and politely expressed, certain statements are unacceptable. To cite a specific example, suppose that the controversial issue in question is the use of nuclear power, a teacher might well decide that the statement by a pupil 'It doesn't bother me if there's a nuclear disaster, so long as it isn't near here' is unacceptable. Racist and sexist views would, similarly, be unacceptable in most circumstances.

Fig. 5.1 Human population and the world's resources.

Teaching about human populations

Possible aims

- Know how the size of the world's population has changed over time.
- Appreciate the concepts of exponential growth and carrying capacity.
- Understand the factors that affect the number of children a family has.
- Realize that issues to do with human population link with such issues as food production, nutrition, aid and development, health and colonialism (Fig. 5.1).
- Describe some of the major differences between countries in population density, population growth rates, birth rates, death rates and infant mortality, and be able to discuss reasons for these differences.

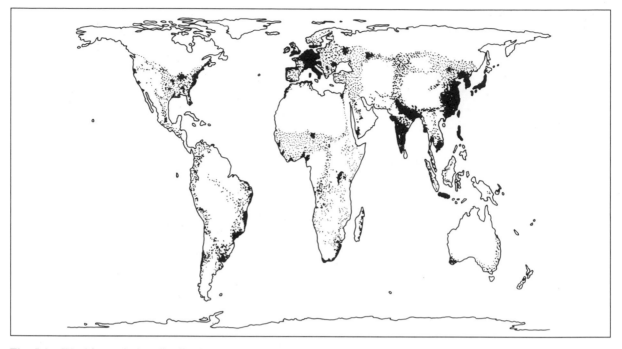

Fig. 5.2   World population distribution. Each dot represents 100 000 people.

Possible teaching approaches

- Plot graphs showing historical changes in world population size.
- Draw maps showing where the world's major concentrations of people are (Fig. 5.2).
- Draw population pyramids.
- Collect data from tombstones on how long people lived at different times in the past.
- Analyse data from obituaries and announcements of deaths in newspapers (e.g. does length of life correlate with gender?).
- Grow duckweed (*Lemna*) in plastic beakers filled with nutrient-rich water, or flour beetles (*Tribolium*) in flour to see population growth curves.
- Role play mother who has four young children and doesn't want any more with father who is worried about who will look after his wife and him in their old age.
- Collect and discuss newspaper and magazine attitudes to population issues.
- Find out the attitude of different religions to family planning.
- Ask members of one's family how many children they would like to have/to have had.

Useful resources

The Population Puzzle and *The Population Puzzle: Teacher's Notes*, ILEA, 1987. Available from Centre for Learning Resources, 275 Kennington Lane, London SE11 5QZ.

Teaching Development Issues: Section 5 – Population Changes, Development Education Project, 1986. Available from DEP, c/o Manchester Polytechnic, 801 Wilmslow Road, Manchester M20 8RG.

How Many Children?, ActionAid, n.d.. Available from ActionAid, Hamlyn House, Archway, London N19 5PG.

World Population Data Sheet. Available from Population Concern, 231 Tottenham Court Road, London W1P 9AE and Population Reference Bureau, 777 14th St, N.W., Suite 800, Washington D.C. 20005, USA.

Many school geography books have valuable material.

Teaching about evolution

Evolution is all too often taught in schools as if it was a fact (i.e. a certainty). Although most scientists would agree that the evidence in favour of evolution is very strong, to teach evolution as a fact does no service to science education and may cause considerable anguish or confusion to some pupils. I have taught more than one A level biology student who didn't accept the theory of evolution, including at least one who got a grade A and went on to read a biological subject at university. I should like to hope that my teaching served not to threaten them, but allowed them to continue to hold their own beliefs while at the same time enabling them to see some of the evidence for evolution and to appreciate the central role the theory of evolution plays in modern biology.

As always when teaching a controversial issue, the attitude of the teacher is so important. With pupils aged approximately 9 to 13 the crucial thing a teacher may be able to do is to show by her attitude and what she says that a conflict model of the relationship between the theory of evolution and religious faith is *not* the only model. With older pupils/students, a wider set of aims and teaching approaches are available.

Possible aims

- Explain the theory of natural selection.
- Distinguish between natural selection and Lamarckianism.
- Describe two examples of natural selection in the wild.
- Outline the evidence for evolution as revealed in the fossil record.
- Outline evidence that the Earth is many millions of years old.
- Discuss difficulties with the theory of evolution.
- Describe the creation stories of at least one religion.
- Explain why some people with a religious faith feel unable to accept the theory of evolution while others can.
- Describe the reception that greeted the publication of Darwin's *The Origin of Species*. . .

Possible learning approaches

- Make fossil casts using plaster of Paris.
- See the consequences of radioactive decay (e.g. radon-220) to appreciate one technique used for dating rocks.
- Make simple sedimentary rocks such as mudstones and sandstones by allowing particles to settle out from a suspension and then allowing water to evaporate.
- Make date-lines using string to show the possible age of the Earth and significant events in its history (1 cm = 10 million years; Earth 4500 million years old; first fossil bacteria 3500 million years ago, etc.).
- Discuss scientific arguments for the incomplete nature of the fossil record (chances of fossils being formed and then discovered are minute; much important evolution may have occurred in small populations over only a few thousand years).
- Discuss difficulties with the theory of evolution (e.g. how did DNA replication get going?; are humans really the product of blind chance?).
- Collate different creation stories (some known by pupils, others by their families, extend through library search).
- Look at arguments by scientists (e.g. Richard Dawkins) suggesting evolution disproves the role of God in creation.
- Look at arguments by scientists and theologians (e.g. John Polkinghorne) suggesting that evolution is compatible with the role of God in creation.
- Look at arguments by creationists (who believe that the evidence in favour of evolution is poor and that the theory of evolution is unacceptable to those with religious faith).
- Role play public reaction shortly after the publication of Darwin's *The Origin of Species* . . .

Useful references and resources

Barbour (1990); Berry (1991); Blackmore and Page (1989); Brooke (1991); Darwin (1859); Dawkins (1986); Heinze (1973); Nasseef and Black (1984); Peacocke (1979); Polkinghorne

(1988); Poole (1990c); Selkirk and Burrows (1987); White (1978).

The journal *Creation* is published by the Creation Science Movement, 50 Brecon Avenue, Portsmouth PO6 2AW.

The journal *Origins* is published by the Biblical Creation Society, PO Box 22, Rugby CV22 7SY.

Teaching about race

Many science teachers will not consider the matter of race as a controversial issue to be discussed in science lessons. They will either not deal with the topic in science lessons or will simply dismiss the notion of human races. There is much to commend in these approaches. As we all know, accepting the existence of distinct human races has more than once led to gross infringements of human rights and even played a part in genocide (e.g. Nazism and the worst excesses of apartheid).

What then might be the reasons for a science teacher wishing to deal with the subject of race in science lessons? Only one, that I can see. Namely that the term is still widely, and I believe appropriately, used when considering variation in species other than our own. In my view a science education for 16-year-olds should include an introduction to the concept of race in non-humans and consider why the term is unhelpful if applied to humans.

Possible aims

- Recognize that in taxonomy race occupies a level in the hierarchy of taxonomic terms beneath that of subspecies.
- Distinguish between variety, race, subspecies and species.
- Explain what are meant by interbreeding, population and gene pool.
- Appreciate that all people are members of the one species *Homo sapiens* and that this species is not split into any constituent subspecies.
- Discuss reasons why the genetic diversity within human populations is greater than the genetic distance between them.

- Explain why humans in different parts of the world show differences in such morphological characteristics as skin colour, body shape, amount of body hair, nose shape and the presence of the sickle cell allele.
- State what are meant by discrete and continuous variation and provide appropriate examples with reference to humans.
- Describe the multiple geographical origins of the people living in any one country.
- Explain how the recognition that humans differ in appearance has led to human rights abuses.

Teaching the issue of race in science lessons

If dealing with race in science lessons, it is important to liaise with one's colleagues, particularly in schools with subject specialists, with colleagues in RE, PSE, geography and history. Care needs to be taken, with pupils and students of whatever age, when dealing with the topic of individual differences. One danger is to overstress individual differences. It is not advisable to analyse results by groups (e.g. gender, skin colour). For one thing, this approach overstates individual differences when a more fruitful approach might be to enable pupils to realize the many similarities between different people. However, the opposite danger is to ignore all individual differences, implicitly pretending that 'we all look the same, don't we?' Such an approach will convince few and fail to uncover any existing or latent racism or sexism. Dealing with racism and sexism are covered in Chapter 4.

Barbara Wyvill (1991) tackles the issue of variation in skin colour head on and suggests that it can be valuable to give pupils access to red, blue, yellow, black and white paints and ask them to mix a paint colour as close as possible to their own skin colour:

> The children may be surprised to find out that all skin colours can be matched by using different proportions of the same paint. 'White' children may be surprised to see how unwhite they are! If each child uses her/his mixed colour to paint a small piece of paper then it will be seen that the colours cannot be put into discrete sets but form a continuous gradation from the lightest to the

Fig. 5.3 The immediate result of an underwater atomic explosion set off by the United States of America in the lagoon off Bikini Atoll on 25 July 1946. The column of water is some 600 m across at its base and 1500 m high.

darkest. This activity can also be used with an 'all white' [*sic*] class to show that, in fact, they are not all the same colour. However, this activity would be inappropriate where there is only a small minority of black or Asian children in the class as it would only reinforce any ideas of the separateness of 'races'.

(Wyvill, 1991: 20–1)

As Wyvill intimates, each teacher has to decide whether such an activity would be helpful or not.

Useful references and addresses

Gill and Levidow (1987); Gould (1981); Rose *et al*. (1984); Thorp (1991); Tomkins (1989); Unesco (1983); Wyvill (1991).

Commission for Racial Equality, Eliot House, 10/12 Allington Street, London SW1E 5EH.

Sickle Cell Society, c/o Brent Community Health Council, 16 High Street, Harlesden, London NW10 4LX.

UK Thalassaemia Society, 107 Nightingale Lane, London N8 7QY.

Teaching about nuclear power

Possible aims

- List the various fuels used to provide electricity and other human requirements.
- Distinguish between renewable and non-renewable energy resources.
- Outline the structure of atoms in terms of electrons and a nucleus of neutrons and protons.
- Explain what are meant by alpha-particle, beta-particle, isotope, fission and chain reaction.
- Explain why so much energy is released in nuclear fission.
- Describe how nuclear fission was discovered.
- Outline the essentials of a nuclear power station.
- Describe what happened in either the Three Mile Island accident or at Chernobyl.
- Discuss the links between the generation of nuclear power and the use of nuclear weapons.
- Outline the principles behind nuclear re-processing.
- Explain how nuclear waste is classified and dealt with.

Possible learning approaches

- Research the roles played by such scientists as Henri Becquerel, Ernest Rutherford, Marie Curie and Lise Meitner.
- Plot a map of the distribution of nuclear power stations around the globe and suggest reasons for the results observed.
- Plot graphs of the decrease in radioactivity in vegetation in Cumbria in the years after Chernobyl and compare the results with government predictions.
- Explain how carbon dioxide emissions from electricity-producing stations in France fell by two-thirds from 1980 to 1987.
- Write to both pro- and anti-nuclear power organizations asking them the same specific questions, e.g. 'How safe is nuclear power?'
- Examine the medical evidence for and against an increase in the incidence of leukaemia around certain nuclear power stations.
- Design and use a questionnaire to investigate fellow pupils' knowledge of and attitudes towards nuclear power.
- Role play a Cabinet meeting trying to decide whether to extend a county's nuclear power programme or to scrap it.
- Write an imaginary letter from one of the servicemen or indigenous people on test islands like Bikini Atoll (Fig. 5.3).

Useful references and addresses

Hawkes (1981); Sang (1990); Wellington (1986).

Bradford University School of Peace Studies, Richmond Road, Bradford BD7 1DP.

British Nuclear Fuels, Risley, Warrington WA3 6AS.

CND (Campaign for Nuclear Disarmament), 22–24 Underwood Street, London N1 7JQ.

Greenpeace, 30–31 Islington Green, London N1 8BR.

NIREX (Nuclear Industry Radioactive Waste Executive), Information Office, Curie Avenue, Harwell, Didcot, OX11 0RH.

United Kingdom Atomic Energy Authority, Information Office, 465 Harwell, Didcot, OX11 0RA.

CHAPTER 6

Life and living processes

Entre le cerveau d'une femme et celui d'un homme il n'y a aucune différence [between the brain of a woman and that of a man there is no difference].

(Jeanne Dumée, 1680, French astronomer)

Life processes and the organization of living things

Surgery

Every culture practises surgery. Trepanation of the skull, an operation to remove a portion of the cranium, may have been performed as long ago as 10 000 BCE. Examples of prehistoric trepanation have been found all over the world. They represent the oldest evidence of surgery. Several techniques are known (e.g. scrapping and cutting) but all involve removing pieces of bone. The rate of survival is indicated by healing processes at the edges of the bone. In the *majority* of cases significant bone regrowth is evident. This contrasts with the success rate in the 1800s in Western Europe when recovery was so unusual that one authority wrote that the first requirement for the operation was 'dass de Wundarzt selbst auf den Kopf gefallen sein müsse' ['that the wound surgeon must himself have fallen on his head'] (Fischer, 1864: 598, cited in Majno, 1991: 28).

By the time of the Fifth Dynasty in Egypt (around 2450 BCE) the use of splints and bandages to set fractured limbs was in practice. The world's oldest medical text is a Sumerian tablet whose style of writing dates it to the Third Dynasty of Ur, c. 2158–2008 BCE or a little earlier. On it are mentioned washing, making plasters and bandaging.

By about 2000 BCE, wound surgery had reached the point in Egypt where there were separate doctors for the eye, the teeth, the belly and the 'hidden diseases'; there was even a 'shepherd of the anus'. By about 1600 BCE medical sutures and tapes are recorded in papyri. Cauterization (use of a red-hot implement to stop bleeding) followed about 100 years later.

The Egyptians of this time were aware of the problems of infection. Malachite or honey was applied to certain wounds, just as myrrh was used in embalming. Recent experiments have shown that ground-up malachite (no doubt because it contains copper), honey and myrrh all prevent the growth of certain bacteria including bacteria of the typhoid-colon group (honey) and *Staphylococcus aureus* (malachite and myrrh). Similar experiments could safely be carried out under school laboratory conditions.

By approximately 400 BCE, apprentice Hindu surgeons were required to undertake a number of experimental procedures for practice (Fig. 6.1). Among the many Indian procedures established at this time was the use of the tourniquet. To India too we owe the earliest treatment of cataracts. For this, a needle is used to push the opaque lens out of the way via an insertion behind the iris. Also first performed in India, as far as we know, were plastic and reconstructive surgery.

Plastic surgery in India probably originated with treatments to ear lobes infected or damaged through the widespread practice of piercing and

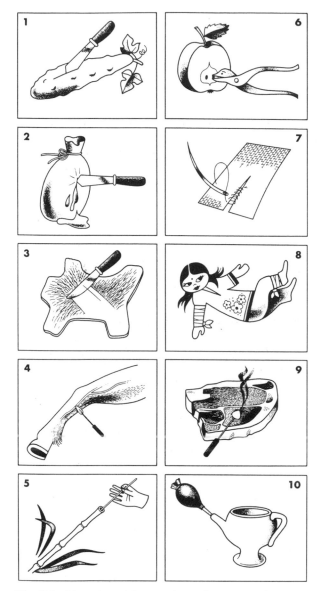

Fig. 6.1 Experimental procedures that apprentice Hindu surgeons were required to practice in approximately 400 BCE.

A description of an ideal Indian hospital dating from around 400 BCE suggests conditions that may not have significantly been improved upon for 2200 years:

> In the first place a mansion must be constructed under the supervision of an engineer . . . It should be spacious and roomy . . . One portion at least should be open to the currents of the wind . . .
>
> It should not be exposed to smoke, or the Sun, or dust, or injurious sound and touch and taste and form and scent . . .
>
> After this should be secured a body of attendants of good behaviour, distinguished for purity and cleanliness of habits, attached to the person for whose service they are engaged, possessed of cleverness and skill, endued with kindness, skilled to every kind of service that a patient may require . . . competent to cook food and curries, clever in bathing or washing a patient . . . or raising the patient or assisting him in walking or moving about, well-skilled in making or cleaning beds, patient and skillful in waiting upon one that is ailing, and never unwilling to do any act that they may be commanded to do . . .
>
> So also should be kept little vessels or cups, larger vessels for washing the hands and face . . . and flatter vessels for holding spittle and evacuations, all placed ready for use, good beds placed upon bedsteads and overlaid with white sheets and containing pillows . . . and diverse kinds of instruments, domestic and surgical.
>
> (Charaka, cited in Majno, 1991: 292–3)

In the tenth century CE, Abu 'Ali al-Husayn bin 'Abdallah bin Sina (generally known in the West as Avicenna) was a physician and prolific writer. One of his books – the *Canon of Medicine* – runs to over a million words. This book points out the importance of diet in health, the influence of climate and the environment on health, the surgical use of oral anaesthetics, the contagious nature of some diseases, and the dangers of diseases spreading via soil and water. Ibn Sina recommended the testing of new drugs by experimentation on animals and humans. He advised surgeons to treat cancer in its earliest stages, making certain surgically to remove all the diseased tissue.

stretching them. Subsequently the techniques were used to reconstruct ears and noses lost in war. For example, a new nose could be built from a flap of skin folded down from the forehead (but, remaining, of course, still partly attached). The flap was of the appropriate shape and the nostrils were moulded over two little tubes.

Personal health

There is a real danger when aspects of health education are taught, whether or not in the context of biology/science lessons, that hidden assumptions appropriate for one culture may be inappropriately, even if unintentionally, transferred to another culture. A classic example is the way many biology textbooks when discussing digestion used to ask pupils to write an essay on 'What happens when I eat a ham sandwich'. Such authors had presumably not considered the point that ham is not permitted as a valid food to Jews, Muslims, vegetarians and vegans. In much the same way, assumptions may be made when teaching sex education that are culturally inappropriate (Reiss, in press).

Munday *et al.* (1989) studied the perceptions of 11–14-year-olds in an ethnically diverse comprehensive school as to what constituted good gum health. A set of six colour photographs were shown to the pupils. These demonstrated pairs of healthy and unhealthy gums with pink, brown and black pigmentation. The pictures were selected to represent a range of ethnic types and to present differences between healthy and unhealthy gums that were apparent to a lay person. Each pupil was individually shown the pictures and was asked by a dental health educator to choose from amongst them those showing gums which were: (a) healthy and (b) unhealthy.

What Munday and her colleagues found was that almost irrespective of their skin colour, 80 per cent of the pupils selected the healthy, pink gums as healthy, whereas fewer than 10 per cent of the pupils selected the healthy, brown or healthy, black gums as healthy. Indeed, the *unhealthy*, pink gums were far more likely to be described as healthy than the healthy, brown or healthy, black ones were. Only one child (a brown-skinned girl) made all the choices correctly. She expressed a wish to train as a dentist. All pupils were subsequently seen in tutor groups and told the 'correct answers'. This information was almost always met with alarm, surprise, disbelief and rejection.

It is clear that pupils would benefit from having teachers who could effectively help them to affirm a view of good health appropriate to their culture and ethnicity. In the same way, teaching about food, despite the fact that food is perhaps the most obvious manifestation of cultural diversity and therefore lends itself to a multicultural approach, can all too often give the impression that the diets favoured by certain groups are unbalanced, or, at best, odd. This latter problem often occurs when pupils are asked to keep food diaries or to log their diets into a piece of software using the language of the teacher or software writer.

Scurvy

In 1535, the French explorer Jacques Cartier overwintered at the Huron village of Hochelaga (modern day Montreal). His men gradually succumbed to scurvy:

> . . . their mouths became stincking, their gummes so rotten, that all the flesh did fall off, even to the rootes of the teeth, which also did fall out . . . about the middle of February, of a hundreth and tenne persons that we were, there were not ten whole . . . There were already eight dead.
>
> (cited by Barker, 1992: 46)

Fortunately for Cartier, the native Americans showed him how to make an infusion from the bark and leaves of the 'Hanneda' tree (possibly the tree known today as the Eastern white cedar, *Thuja occidentalis*). The effects were remarkable. As Cartier wrote:

> . . . if all the phisicians of Montpellier and Lovaine had been there with all the drugs in Alexandria they would not have done so much in one yere as that tree did in six days.
>
> (cited by Barker, 1992: 46)

Over the next two hundred years, a million European sailors died from scurvy until a cure for the disease was 'discovered' by the Scot James Lind and adopted by another Scot, Gilbert Blane, and others. Even in the nineteenth century, there was an editorial in the *London Medical Gazette* doubting the value of lemon juice to prevent or cure scurvy: 'it has long been known to many intelligent observers that . . . lemon juice is by no means an infallible cure for scurvy' (Budd,

Fig. 6.2 Assyrian bas-relief from the seventh century BCE showing that it was known that damage to the spinal cord may result in paralysis of the hind legs.

1842: 634, cited by Carpenter, 1986: 235). With hindsight, part of the problem seems to have been the variable quality of the lemon juice used. Another complicating factor is that whereas it was the ships' surgeons who came into contact with cases of scurvy, they were socially inferior to the land-based physicians who, although much less likely to have had any first-hand experience of the disease, were much more likely to write about it!

The nervous system

A famous Assyrian bas-relief dating from the seventh century BCE shows a lioness with her hind legs paralysed as a result of arrow injuries to her spinal cord (Fig. 6.2). By approximately 400 BCE,

though the dating is very uncertain, the treatises of Sushrutu were written in India. Within them they include an analysis of the three things that could happen if an arrow or other pointed weapon plunged into the neck. Translated into modern anatomical terms: if the glossopharyngeal nerve is severed, the sense of taste is lost; if Galen's recurrent laryngeal nerve is severed, the ability to speak is almost lost; if the vagus nerve is severed, the ability to speak is almost lost.

Uses of enzymes and microbes – baking, brewing and dairy industries

Unleavened bread in various forms (comparable to modern-day chapatis) was probably being made by 10 000 BCE (see p. 74 on agriculture). In a science lesson it probably helps learning if chapatis (which do not require the carbon dioxide respired by yeast) are made before leavened bread is.

Archaeological evidence reveals that by 6000 BCE, a type of acid beer was being made with yeast in Egypt. By the second millennium BCE, the Sumerians brewed at least 19 brands of beer – a whole book on the subject survives. A project is currently underway at the National Institute of Agricultural Botany in Cambridge to grow emmer wheat (*Triticum dicoccum*). This wheat still grows wild in the Middle East. Archaeological excavations show that this was the wheat used for brewing in a bakery-cum-brewery believed to have been built by Akhenaton, Tutankhamen's father. The plan is to brew an experimental Pharaohs' beer. The brewers Scottish and Newcastle have expressed an interest in possible commercial developments.

It is likely that yogurt (from the Turkish word *jugurt*) was made by the nomadic tribes of the Middle East who kept such milk-producing animals as cows, sheep, goats and camels. Remnants of cheese have been found in the tomb of Hories-Aha, dated around 3000 BCE.

Circulation of the blood

The circulation of the blood in humans was known to the Chinese by the second century BCE at the latest, when it is described in *The Yellow Emperor's Manual of Corporeal Medicine*. Two separate circulations of fluids were envisaged. Blood, pumped by the heart, flowed through the vascular system. *Ch'i*, an ethereal, rarefied form of energy, was pumped by the lungs to circulate the body in invisible tracts. The notion of a dual circulation was central to the practice of acupuncture.

The Chinese carried out studies which involved removing blood vessels from corpses, stretching them out to their full length and working out the total distance traversed by the blood in one circuit. As *The Yellow Emperor's Manual* says:

What we call the vascular system is like dykes and retaining walls forming a circle of tunnels which

control the path that is traversed by blood so that it cannot escape or find anywhere to leak away.

(cited in Temple, 1991: 123–4)

The pulmonary circulation was discovered by Ibn Nafīs, the Islamic scientist who died in 1288. In his *The Epitome of the Canon* he writes:

When the blood has been refined in the Right Ventricle, it needs be that it pass to the Left Ventricle where the Vital Spirit is generated. But between these two there exists no passage. For the substance of the heart there is solid and there exists neither a visible passage, as some writers have thought, nor an invisible passage which will permit the flow of blood, as Galen believed. But on the contrary the pores of the heart are shut and its substance there is thick. But this blood, after being refined, must of necessity pass along the Pulmonary Artery into the lungs to spread itself out there and to mix with the air until the last drop be purified. It then passes along the Pulmonary Veins to reach the Left Ventricle of the Heart after mixing with the air in order to become fit to generate the Vital Spirit. The remainder of the blood, less refined, is used in the nutrition of the lungs. That is why there are between these two passages (i.e., the Pulmonary Arteries and Veins) perceptible passages.

(cited in Nasr, 1987: 213–14)

In the late eighteenth century, Mrs Hutton, a botanist and pharmacist who lived in Shropshire, started to use extracts from the plant foxglove (*Digitalis*) for the treatment of heart disease. In 1785 she sold her recipe to Dr William Withering who is usually credited with the discovery. The drug digitalis is still widely used for the same purpose.

Endocrinology

By the second century BCE the Chinese were isolating sex and pituitary hormones from human urine and using them for medicinal purposes. In Europe the discovery that the urine of pregnant women was rich in sex hormones was made in 1927. Subsequently it was found that the urine contains pituitary gonadotrophins, which stimulate the gonads. Today the derivation of sex hormones from human urine is a standard practice, used for example, in the manufacture of fertility drugs.

The Chinese were well aware of the large amounts of urine needed. For example, a recipe from 1025 requires the use of over 150 gallons, from which it is said that two or three ounces of the crystals will result. The procedures used were chemically most sophisticated and included sublimation and the use of gypsum and other substances to precipitate the hormones out of urine. By examining the published recipes, it is clear that the methods used resulted in the extraction of hormones contaminated by substances which would have had little effect on their biological efficacy. It hardly needs to be said that great care was taken as to whether the hormones were obtained from men or from women. Among the conditions treated were hypogonadism, impotence, sex reversals, hermaphroditism, spermatorrhoea and dysmenorrhoea. Although hormones are, of course, far less effective when taken orally (as they were by the Chinese) than when injected, the Chinese seem to have taken such large doses that it is thought that they would have been at least partially effective.

By the seventh century CE, at the latest, the Chinese were using thyroxine to treat goitre. The physician Chen Ch'uan, who died in 643 CE, recommended in his book *Old and New Tried and Tested Prescriptions* that the physician wash a hundred thyroid glands obtained from gelded rams, remove the fat, chop them up and mix with jujube dates. They should then be made into pills to be swallowed by the patient. Environmental causes of goitre were known by the Chinese from the third century BCE, and seaweed (high in iodine) was used as a treatment for the condition.

Diabetes

It is not known when the Chinese first recognized the symptoms of diabetes, but in the seventh century CE one Chinese physician wrote:

> This disease is due to weakness of the renal and urogenital system. In such cases the urine is always

sweet. Many physicians do not recognise this symptom . . . the cereal foods of the farmers are the precursors of sweetness.

> (Li Hsuan, cited in Temple, 1991: 133)

The sweetness of the urine of diabetics was also known to the Indians, though the relevant texts cannot be dated with any certainty. In the West the sweetness of the urine of diabetics was first noted by Thomas Willis in about 1660.

Insulin

Davidson Nicol was born in 1924 in Freetown, Sierra Leone. He went to Cambridge University as an undergraduate and got a First Class degree. He applied to London Hospital Medical College to become a cardiologist. Initially he was accepted, but when the cardiology consultant saw that he was black, he turned him down, thus ending Nicol's hopes of becoming a cardiologist. However, Nicol managed to get accepted by a physiologist and in 1959, back at Cambridge University, succeeded in working out the chemical structure of insulin.

Penicillin, vitamin B$_{12}$ and insulin

Dorothy Hodgkin was born in 1910 in Cairo and her early education was in the Middle East and Africa. As a teenager she was attracted by both archaeology and chemistry, eventually choosing to study the latter at Oxford University. In the 1930s she was one of the first people to use and develop the techniques of X-ray crystallography. Her major research triumphs included the determination of the three-dimensional structures of penicillin, vitamin B$_{12}$ and insulin. Her work has led to a better understanding of the functioning of these compounds, and has been of considerable medical importance. In 1964 she received the Nobel Prize, an event described by at least one British tabloid newspaper as 'Housewife wins Nobel Prize!'. In 1965 she became the first woman to receive the British Order of Merit since Florence Nightingale. She was Chancellor of Bristol University from 1970 to 1988.

Blood transfusions

Charles Drew was an Afro-American doctor who invented blood banks. He was born in 1904 in a ghetto in Washington, D.C. In 1933 he received his Master of Surgery and Doctor of Medicine degrees. During the Second World War, Drew was approached by the British government and asked to start a blood bank programme for use on the battlefield. This he did. It was so successful that he was asked to organize an international blood bank project and to become the first Director of the American Red Cross Blood Bank.

Although he received many awards and honours, Drew experienced racism all his life. In 1941, he resigned his position with the American Red Cross Blood Bank after it was decided that blood from black donors should not be mixed with blood from white donors. In 1950 Drew was seriously injured in a car accident in North Carolina. He needed a blood transfusion but the hospital he was rushed to refused to treat him because he was black. Drew died before reaching a hospital that would treat him.

Developmental biology

Ernest Everett Just (1883–1941) was a black scientist who started his career in the USA. In the face of debilitating racist experiences he spent more and more time working in Europe during the years before the outbreak of the Second World War. Here he did his most important research, studying the role played by cell surfaces in development. However, his wife, whom he married in 1939, was part-Jewish and the two of them had to flee occupied France. They returned to the USA where Just died soon after.

Animal behaviour

The work of Jane Goodall on chimpanzees, Dian Fossey on gorillas and Fiona Guinness on red deer are discussed on pp. 21–23.

Sarah Blaffer Hrdy (born 1946) produced in 1977 the definitive study of the behaviour of the sacred hanuman langur of North India in her book *The Langurs of Abu*. Along with many other sociobiologists, Blaffer Hrdy looked separately at the strategies used by males and females. Sporadic reports of infanticide in a number of species of monkey had been reported in the literature. Blaffer Hrdy was able to show the extent of this behaviour among adult male hanuman langurs. Such males routinely kill the offspring sired by *other* males. Over evolutionary time, such behaviour has been favoured by natural selection as it causes the female to come into heat again – what else can she do? – so that, from the male's point of view, he gets to reproduce sooner. Blaffer Hrdy wasn't content to portray female langurs as helpless victims. She revealed that females have a number of strategies to help prevent their offspring from being killed. One is that they can show post-coital oestrous behaviour and mate with other males. That is, a female may attempt, sometimes successfully, to *deceive* a male into thinking that he is the father of her next offspring, when in fact he isn't.

Jeanne Altmann has worked for many years on primate behaviour, despite having a degree in mathematics. Among her early work was a most important paper published in 1974. This set new standards for the precision with which behavioural data needed to be collected and analysed. In 1980 she produced *Baboon Mothers and Infants*, the fruit of a long-term study of yellow baboons, initiated by her husband Stuart Altmann, in the Amboseli National Park, Kenya. This book was unique for setting first-rate behavioural data within a rigorous mathematical framework. In this way, for example, Altmann was able to look at how much extra time lactating baboons have to spend foraging by considering the energetic demands of their infants, a question that may have been particularly interesting to a human mother working long hours in the field.

Monoclonal antibodies

Cesar Milstein was born in 1927 in Argentina. He lived there until moving to Cambridge University in 1963. In 1975, with G. Köhler, he devised a way of making monoclonal antibodies. Such antibodies belong to a clone, and so are genetically identical.

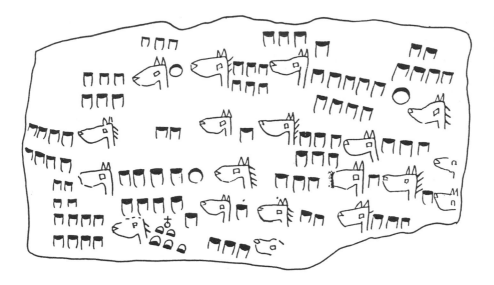

Fig. 6.3 Tablet from Elam dating from around 3000 BCE and showing breeding records.

They have a great many uses within medicine. For example, poisons can be attached to specific monoclonal antibodies directed against tumours. This is known as the 'magic bullet' method of cancer treatment and is currently being very actively researched. Milstein, Köhler and another scientist shared the Nobel prize for physiology in 1984.

Variation and the mechanisms of inheritance and evolution

Fossils

Mary Anning (1799–1847) was a British palaeontologist who lived and worked at Lyme Regis. She made several important palaeontological finds including the first complete ichthyosaur skeleton, a plesiosaur and a pterodactyl. Many histories of geology ignore or understate her role in the development of the science. Even the fossils she found, which currently reside in many of the world's leading collections, often bear not her name, but the names of those who purchased her finds. In 1991 the Lyme Regis Museum, built on the site of the house where she was born, launched an international appeal for funds to return the fossil gallery to its former glory; £100000 is needed

to display the fossils as they would have been in a Victorian fossil hunter's study. By September 1992 approximately £50000 had been raised. (Donations can be sent to The Lyme Regis Museum Appeal, Lyme Regis (Philpot) Museum, Lyme Regis, Dorset, ST7 3QA, UK.)

Selective breeding

Genetics may be a much older science than is generally realized. Figure 6.3 shows a sketch of a clay tablet dating from about 3000 BCE. The tablet is from Elam (now in south-western Iran) and appears to show a breeding record of what may have been domesticated donkeys. Notice the various types of mane. The script is known as proto-Elamite and has not yet been deciphered.

Pupils often hear about the possible problems of genetic uniformity among crops – a consequence of the current domination of the world's agricultural markets by a few very large multinationals. It may help pupils to realize the consequences that too much genetic uniformity among crops may have if they know that this is not a modern phenomenon. There is good evidence that genetic uniformity was one of the major contributing factors to the devastating Irish potato famine of 1845–9. The famine resulted in the starvation of over a million people and the emigration to the

USA of about one-and-a-half million – and that from a population of only nine million people.

Unlike their counterparts in the Andes, where the potato was domesticated over 8000 years ago and where numerous varieties of potato are grown, the Irish grew potatoes descended from only a few clones introduced from England and mainland Europe. These in turn were the result of just two samples of potatoes brought from South America to Spain in 1570 and to England around 1590. In the Irish potato famine, potato ·blight, caused by the protoctist *Phytophthera infestans*, spread like wildfire. In the Andes, the mixture of different natural varieties – known as landraces – provided some protection against the disease.

Throughout the years of the Irish potato famine, Irish farmers continued successfully to produce cereals, cattle, pigs, eggs and butter. Enough food was produced to ensure that no one in Ireland need have starved. However, farmers had to export these crops to England to get the money they needed to pay the rents they owed their English landlords. Farmers who failed to export their produce were evicted from their farms and had their cottages razed to the ground.

It is even possible that the genetic uniformity of crop plants may have played a part in the collapse of the Mayan civilization in Mexico. In Mexico, increases in the human population led to the intensification of agriculture from around 500 CE. The traditional pattern of slash-and-burn farming gave way to extensive terracing of slopes and reclamation of formerly untilled swamp land for agriculture. Maize (corn) became the dominant food and year-in, year-out production may have facilitated the build-up of pests. Successive outbreaks of maize mosaic virus transmitted by corn-leaf hoppers probably led to a collapse in maize production and may well have contributed to the demise of the Mayas and their conquest by the Toltecs in about 900 CE.

In 1977 Rafael Guzmán, a botany student at the University of Guadalajara in Mexico, discovered a wild relative of maize new to science – *Zea diploperennis*. Plants of this new species have now been shown to be immune to, or tolerant of, seven of the nine tropical viral diseases of maize. For three of these diseases, *Zea diploperennis* is the only source of viral immunity. This may prove to be of great commercial value as some of the viruses cause economically important diseases.

Naming organisms

Background

Most biology textbooks for use with pupils over the age of about 13, or with students, extol the value of the binomial system of nomenclature. This method of naming organisms was devised by the Swede Carl von Linné (1707–78), usually known by the Latin version of his name, Carl Linnaeus. By the time he died he had given binomial names to over 8500 plants and to some 4400 animals (Mann and Vivian, 1963). Subsequently, his work has been continued so that practically all known species, whether extant or extinct, are given binomial names.

There is not the slightest doubt that the binomial system of nomenclature is a tremendous help to professional biologists who have to communicate with their colleagues in other countries. Consider what is sometimes described as Britain's national bird – the robin. Its Linnaean name is *Erithacus rubecula*. This name holds in all countries, whereas in France the robin is known as 'le rouge-gorge', in Germany as 'das Rotkehlchen', in Spain as 'el petirrojo', in Italy as 'il pettirosso', etc.

Another advantage of the Linnaean system is seen from the fact that the word robin in the USA is given to a recognizably different bird – whose Linnaean name is *Turdus migratorius*. Similarly, in New Zealand robin is the name given to various birds in the genus *Miro*; in Australia to species of *Petroica*; and in Jamaica it is another name for the green tody. Further, the name *Erithacus rubecula* will not change over time, unless a change is formally agreed according to strict rules of nomenclature. On the other hand, in Britain the following alternative spellings are all cited in the *Oxford English Dictionary*: robyn, roben, robene, robeen, robein, robbin.

However, even within the academic community, the universal adoption of the binomial system has been criticized by certain palaeontologists (Hughes, 1989; Chapman, 1992). These criticisms centre on the impossibility of recognizing whether or not two fossils belong to the same species (defined by the ability to interbreed), and should therefore be given the same binominal name. These problems are especially acute when fossil plants are being studied, as different people often work on the different parts of plants (e.g. pollen versus leaves versus woods), all of which therefore end up being given different Latin names.

At school level, a quite different criticism can be levelled at the universal adoption of the binomial system: it denigrates the knowledge that pupils bring to their lessons. Practically every biology textbook asserts that the binomial system is 'better' than other methods (this assertion is so ubiquitous that selected citations would be invidious).

It is extremely important to emphasize that the question, 'What is the best system for naming organisms?', cannot unequivocally be answered. Indeed, it can be argued that the question, while an important one, lies outside the domain of science. Academic botanists have their reasons for preferring a binomial system. Fair enough. For those people who don't know any classical Latin (i.e. something in excess of 99 per cent of all pupils), a vernacular system immediately commends itself.

People name organisms for all sorts of reasons, not just to acknowledge whether or not the organisms belong to different biological species. All humans have a propensity to name organisms. Indeed, anthropological studies regularly show that native people have exceptionally detailed knowledges of their local flora and fauna. For instance, in a study carried out by Russell-Smith and published in 1985, four Aboriginal people speaking the Mayiali language were able to identify and name some 420 different plants. For each plant, there was a detailed knowledge of its season of flowering, its habitat, whether or not parts were edible or poisonous and what could be made from it. In several cases the plants had not yet been named and described using the binomial system (cited by Hiatt and Rhys Jones, 1988).

The way in which the traditional naming of organisms may differ from that given under the binomial system, with the central role played there by the concept of the biological species, is illuminating. Hiatt and Rhys Jones (1988) give the example of the Gidjingarli-speaking people of the Blyth River in Australia:

In general, Gidjingarli names for plants in their environment correspond to scientific species. Thus there are different names for jabiru, brolga, magpie goose, burdekin duck, grass whistle duck, black duck, pelican, and so on. All these birds form part of the diet. However, many small birds, especially those seen fleetingly in rainforest patches, are given a collective term *badaitja*, the best translation being 'small bird'. *Badaitja* have no economic value. However, some birds that are not part of the normal diet do have proper names. These birds play important roles in totemic song cycles; their habits, or characteristics such as distinctive plumage or song, are depicted on bark or body paintings, or enacted in dance and song.

For the economically most important animals, the Gidjingarli subdivide within the species. Thus in the case of both the agile wallaby (*M. agilis*) and the kangaroo (*M. antilopinus*), the male and the female are given separate names. The Gidjingarli know perfectly well that they are of the same biological species. In the case of the barramundi (*Lates calcarifer*), different stages in its life-cycle are given different names. The silvery coloured young fish moving in from the sea at the beginning of the wet season are called *anamutjala*, whereas the older, larger and dark coloured fish speared or trapped on the estuarine wetlands at the end of the wet season are called *djanambal*. Again the Gidjingarli realize they are dealing with the same species; indeed, their knowledge of the life-cycles of this and other estuarine/wetland fish is profound and accurate. . .

The Gidjingarli see each taxon as an immutable entity, enshrined in the totemic religious system. Many are said to 'have a song', that is, they form part of the great song cycles, which relate them to the other elements of the panoply – land and people. Some taxa have secret ('inside') names used only in ceremonies and usually with restricted access as to their true meaning.

(Hiatt and Rhys Jones, 1988: 5–6)

The control that some scientists want to have over the naming of organisms has even spread to the point where committees are appointed to agree on non-Linnaean names! This has already happened to British native plants and is now beginning to happen to British birds (Clover, 1992).

The bird changes are being finalized by a committee of the International Ornithological Congress. Under its proposals, the stone curlew would become the Eurasian thick knee, the red grouse would become the willow ptarmigan and Bewick's swan would become the tundra swan. (Bewick's swan was named in 1830 in honour of the illustrator Thomas Bewick (1755–1828) who first distinguished it from the whooper swan. Bewick worked almost exclusively as a woodblock engraver. This technique is thought to have been invented by the thirteenth century Italians – Alexander Cunio and his twin sister Isabella.)

Many other of the most familiar British birds would have their names slightly changed – the wren, for instance, would become the winter wren and the robin would become the European robin. In a quotation which would not be out of place in George Orwell's *1984*, Dr Alan Knox, Chair of the British Ornithological Union's Records Committee, the body which is handling the changes in Britain, defended the proposed changes, saying:

> There have always been three kinds of name for birds: the scientific name, the English name and the common name. Most of the general public will not ever come into contact with the English names. They will pass them by. They will use the common names.
>
> (Clover, 1992: 2)

Possible teaching strategy

A good biological education, certainly for most pupils aged 14 and over, should indeed include an introduction to the binomial system of nomenclature. But it should also include an account of traditional methods of naming organisms. The fundamental point is that people give names to the organisms that are *significant* for them. Pupils could be encouraged to realize what names they and other members of their families give to which

organisms and why. These reasons may include: food purposes; reasons to do with employment, economy and health (farming, economic pests, disease-causing organisms); reasons of relaxation and enjoyment (gardening, bird watching, fishing, pets); and religious/cultural reasons (food taboos).

Structure of DNA

By now the role played by Rosalind Franklin in the elucidation of the structure of DNA is generally well known. However, the way most people still interpret her work is through the eyes of James Watson's *The Double Helix*. This is perhaps the most readable account ever written by a scientist of their work. However, in it Rosalind Franklin does not come across very well. Although in an epilogue Watson admits 'my initial impressions of her, both scientific and personal (as recorded in the early pages of this book), were often wrong' (Watson, 1970: 175), it is his initial impressions that most people remember.

For example, throughout his book Watson maintains that Rosalind Franklin was 'caught in her self-made antihelical trap' (*ibid.*: 164). In fact, as Franklin's friend and biographer, Anne Sayre, has shown from an examination of Franklin's lecture notes, Franklin had argued in favour of a helical structure since at least 1951, two years before Watson and Crick made their discovery of the structure of DNA. Franklin's personality and behaviour don't come across much better in Watson's account either:

> Suddenly Rosy came from behind the lab bench that separated us and began moving towards me. Fearing that in her hot anger she might strike me, I grabbed up the Pauling manuscript and hastily retreated to the open door. My escape was blocked by Maurice [Wilkins], who, searching for me, had just then stuck his head through . . . Walking down the passage, I told Maurice how his unexpected appearance might have prevented Rosy from assaulting me.
>
> (Watson, 1970: 131–2)

Rosalind Franklin died of cancer on 16 April 1958, aged 37. In 1962 Francis Crick, James Watson and Maurice Wilkins shared the Nobel prize for Physiology. (Nobel Prizes cannot be awarded posthumously and cannot be shared by more than three people.)

Jumping genes

Barbara McClintock was born in 1902 and died in 1992. During the 1940s she found a group of mutations in maize that failed to behave in the way expected by classical genetics. The implications of McClintock's work were not appreciated by the rest of the scientific community for many years, but in 1983 she was awarded a Nobel Prize. Her research demonstrated the existence of so-called 'jumping genes' – pieces of DNA that can move from one chromosome to another. Now that the principles of genetic engineering are commonplace, such an idea may not seem so extraordinary. At the time, however, it was so strange that it simply didn't fit into the existing paradigm and so was ignored for many years.

Elucidation of the genetic code

Har Gobind Khorana (born in 1922) was educated in the Punjab before moving to England and then the USA. He synthesized the 64 possible base sequences that can be made from the four bases that constitute a codon of messenger RNA. This allowed the elucidation of the genetic dictionary which shows how triplets of bases in DNA code for particular amino acids, and so determine the protein made by a gene. Khorana was awarded the Nobel Prize in 1968.

Evidence for evolution

See pp. 59–60 on evolution.

Populations and human influences within ecosystems

Human population size

Human population size is covered on pp. 57–8. Perhaps here, though, I can make a point about the best sort of map projection to use when visually presenting evidence about the distribution of populations or anything else in different parts of the world.

It is the case that no two-dimensional projection (i.e. a flat map) can faithfully represent both the shape and the area of different parts of the world. One or both must be distorted. Now geographers often have very good reasons for wanting some sort of compromise projection, that is one which distorts both shape (i.e. directions) and area, but distorts each as little as possible. It can be argued though, that for scientists, particularly biologists, an accurate representation of area is usually far more important than an accurate representation of shape. This is because scientists are interested in such things as population densities (i.e. number of organisms *per unit area*), the distribution of biomes, etc. Several different equal area projections are available. The best known is Peters, though academic geographers generally prefer Eckert IV or Hammer.

The agricultural revolution

The domestication of animals and plants seems to have happened independently around 10000 to 8000 BCE in the Middle East, the Orient and the Americas.

Around 10000 to 9000 BCE, the dog was domesticated in Mesopotamia and Canaan. Within a thousand years goats and sheep were domesticated in Persia (modern-day Iran) and Afghanistan, and emmer wheat and barley were being cultivated in Canaan. Around 8000 to 7000 BCE, potatoes and beans were domesticated in Peru, rice in Indochina and pumpkins in middle America. Floodwater agriculture was developed in the Nile valley and in south-western Asia.

By 6000 BCE, the pig and water buffalo had been domesticated in eastern Asia and China, the chicken in southern Asia and cattle in southeastern Anatolia (modern-day Turkey). At the same time, einkorn wheat was being cultivated in Syria, durm (macaroni) wheat in Anatolia, sugarcane in New Guinea, yams, bananas and coconuts in Indonesia, flax in south-western Asia and maize and peppers in the Tehuacan valley of Mexico.

It is worth emphasizing just what is involved in the farming of domesticated animals or plants:

Breeding of animals or sowing of seeds.
Caring for the animals or plants.
Collecting produce (e.g. harvesting, milking, slaughtering).
Selecting and keeping back some of the produce for the next generation.

The important point is that every society has now and always has had ways of feeding its members. Of course, not all societies are agricultural, but every society has means of obtaining food from its environment and of living in relationship with its environment. What can in schools become the rather boring rote-learning of the development of the plough or the evolution of polyploidy in wheat can be made far more personal and interesting if pupils are helped to find out for themselves how food can be obtained. If a school has an outside plot of cultivated land or greenhouse or keeps animals for rural studies, then the possibilities for experimental work are endless.

Biological control

In 304 CE, Hsi Han in his *Records of the Plants and Trees of the Southern Regions* describes how carnivorous ants are used as a biological means of pest control:

> The mandarin orange is a kind of orange with an exceptionally sweet and delicious taste . . . The people of Chiao-Chih sell in their markets ants in bags of rush matting. The nests are like silk. The bags are all attached to twigs and leaves, which, with the ants inside the nests, are for sale. The ants are reddish-yellow in colour, bigger than ordinary ants. These ants do not eat the oranges, but attack and kill the insects which do. In the south, if the mandarin orange trees do not have this kind of ant, the fruits will be damaged by many harmful insects, and not a single fruit will be perfect.
>
> (Temple, 1991: 94–5)

Precisely the same procedure continues to this day.

Introduced species

If not careful, it is all-too-easy for teachers in one country (e.g. England) to give the impression that the problem of introduced species is one of 'their' introduced species causing havoc with 'our' native ones. A large article in *The Independent on Sunday* of 17 May 1992 had the headline 'The barbarians in Britain's back yards'. The accompanying sub-heading read 'Ferocious, fast-growing foreign plants and weeds now pose a serious threat to our countryside' (Schoon, 1992: 7). Replace 'plants and weeds' with 'Jews' and you have a fitting piece of 1930s Nazi propaganda. Similarly, an article in the autumn 1992 issue of *Natural World* was titled 'Unwelcome visitors' with a sub-heading 'Barbara Donne advises closing the door to foreign intruders' (Donne, 1992).

Julian Agyeman has written about the value of introduced species in the urban environment and introduces the term 'multicultural ecosystems'. A different approach is to recognize that introductions can often damage native flora and fauna, but to emphasize the international nature of the problem. Examples include the Nile perch in Lake Victoria, pigs, goats and rats on the many islands and rabbits in Australia. Nile perch were introduced into Lake Victoria in the 1950s by white colonists. They are voracious predators (the perch, that is), growing to 200 kg. It is thought that the introduction of the perch may have been responsible for the fact that many species of local fish have drastically declined in numbers and may be going extinct. As Lake Victoria provides food and work for a million people in Kenya, Tanzania and Uganda, the potential harm caused by this introduction is huge.

Habitat destruction

It is too easy to give the impression that habitat destruction is the fault of non-Western countries – the destruction of the rain forests, for instance. There are at least three ways out of this. One is to look at *why* tropical rain forests are being cut down or burned. Reasons include: clearing land for cattle grazing, the meat from which goes to Western consumers; export of tropical hard woods; planting of cash crops which are exported to generate foreign currency much of which is then used to repay loans; systematic genocide of indigenous peoples. A second is to enable pupils to realize that when non-Western countries destroy forests, they are simply doing what Western countries have already done. England, for instance, is one of the least wooded countries in the world. (I happen to live in Cambridgeshire which is the least wooded county in England.) A third is to realize that, while Western countries aren't *directly* responsible for the clearance of tropical rain forests, they are still destroying a great many natural habitats. Typical examples in Britain include the drainage of meadowland, the extraction of peat, the 'reclamation' of estuarine environments and the planting of non-native conifers on heathland and in the Flow Country.

It is important to avoid giving the impression that people in non-Western countries are always helpless victims. The story of the Chipko Movement is an inspiring example of how a group of women have peacefully collaborated to stop the destruction of forests in their region and start a major tree-planting programme. The forests of the Himalayas are very important to the villagers who live in the foothills. They depend on the trees for such things as firewood for cooking, fodder for their animals and a source of building materials. However, the slow growing sal, deodar and oak are highly prized commercially and much of the forest has been felled for non-local exploitation.

Without these broad-leaved trees, the humus that used to act as a sponge and absorb the monsoon rains is scarcer. In consequence, floods are more frequent and heavier, and erosion and landslides have become problems. On 20 July 1970, a fierce storm struck the Alaknanda valley and in the resulting flood there were many deaths. Relief workers and local people organized marches, following the Gandhian tradition of non-violent protest, and demanded the cessation of commercial logging and the return of forest control to local people.

Despite all this, commercial logging continued and in March 1974 the women organized vigilante parties to keep watch for any axemen. When

axemen approached a tree, the women would surround and embrace the trees, protecting them. 'Chipko' means 'embrace' and so the Chipko Movement was born. Hundreds of women took a pledge to save the trees at the cost of their lives. Over the next few years auctions to sell off areas of land for logging had to be cancelled and the forests were saved.

Subsequently, the Chipko Movement began to afforest deforested areas with native species. Again, this has been organized and implemented by women. Since 1981 the Movement has spread to other areas of India. For further details see the *Chipko Education Pack* listed under 'Education packs and series' in the Resources on p. 115.

Pollution

Some sorts of pollution are a universal human phenomenon – sewage, for example. In rural areas the density of people is such that sewage is rarely a major problem as far as pollution goes, though it may be a health problem. It is when human population density is high that sewage becomes a major pollutant. Many pollutants, though, are mostly produced in the West, carbon dioxide for example (Fig. 6.4).

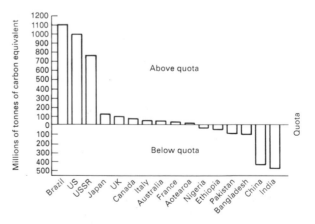

Fig. 6.4 An attempt to quantify the contribution of different countries to carbon dioxide pollution. Brazil comes out worse because of its combination of forest burning and heavy industrial pollution. Otherwise, all the worst offenders are Northern Industrial countries.

Energy flows and cycles of matter within ecosystems

Decay and the preservation of foods

The topic of food preservation lends itself to a multicultural approach. Pupils should be able to suggest a variety of ways in which foods have traditionally been preserved. This list will probably be extended if members of their families are asked to name others. The most likely to be suggested are: drying, salting, curing/smoking, pickling, making into jams, freezing, canning and cooking. From such a list it is then easy to teach that decay requires the presence of decay organisms, water and oxygen. Multicultural science needs to value all forms of indigenous science. So, if, for example, the lesson is taking place in a mainly white school, it is important that such traditional native methods as jam making are considered as well as other apparently more exotic solutions.

Most of these approaches to food preservation lend themselves to experimental investigation. Making edible jam that won't go mouldy for months or longer is not trivial!

Essentially the same tactics used in food preservation are used in embalming. The differences are due partly to the fact that the embalmer's work, unlike that of the cook's, does not have to remain edible. On the other hand, an embalmer has to ensure that the deceased looks as much as possible as they did before death, whereas no one expects a kipper to look like a herring.

The embalmers in Egypt in the first and second millennia BCE used natural soda, a mixture of sodium carbonate and bicarbonate. They removed most of the viscera and inserted little packages of natron. The whole body was then covered with natron and possibly left to dry in the sun. Bacteria and other decomposers are killed by natron which works in much the same way that modern mothballs do. Finally, the body was treated with resins, especially frankincense and myrrh.

CHAPTER 7

Materials and their properties

People all over the world are involved in chemical processes whether they be making soap and candles, purifying salt, brewing beer or wine, spreading fertilizers and weedkillers, washing clothes, bleaching hair, applying suntan lotion, developing films, glueing joints, patching an old car with fibreglass, or a host of other activities carried out for pleasure, profit or self-preservation.

(Williams, 1984: 135)

The properties, classification and structure of materials

Different cultures have known about the properties of different materials since long before recorded history. For example, we know almost nothing in any detail of the early history of dyes, except that many thousands of years ago, every culture made and used them. As the quote by Williams at the head of this chapter indicates, chemistry cannot help but be multicultural.

Metallurgy

The lower half of the reactivity series – iron, lead, tin, copper, silver, gold – is the reverse of the order in which people isolated these metals before and during the Copper, Bronze and Iron Ages. At first all metals were obtained, not by smelting, but from relatively pure veins or nuggets. Iron was exceptionally valuable as it was obtained from meteorites.

Until recently, archaeologists called the first metal age the Bronze Age. It is now known that before bronze was ever made, there was a long period when smelted coppers were used. For example, the Iceman discovered on 19 September 1991 by Helmut and Erika Simon in the Similaun glacier on the Austrian–Italian border had a copper axe. Radiocarbon dating showed that the

body was approximately 5300 years old and thus came from the Copper Age, as the Bronze Age in this area did not start for another thousand years.

Copper can be obtained from copper oxide by direct reduction in the presence of charcoal. The earliest copper artefacts made in this way – a spatula, an awl and a chisel - date from 3800 BCE and come from Yahya (Iran). The ability to extract copper from sulphide ores followed quickly.

Bronze is an alloy of copper and tin. The hardest sort of bronze contains about 10 per cent tin. Bronze can be made in two ways. The first is by adding metallic tin to molten copper. It is more likely that bronze was usually made by mixing cassiterite (the natural form of tin(IV) oxide, SnO_2) with copper, and heating to the melting point of bronze. At this point cassiterite is reduced to tin and absorbed by the copper. Tin sulphide, stannite, can also be used in this way.

The earliest bronzes come from the early city states of Mesopotamia and date from 3000–2500 BCE. The hardness of bronze made it a valuable metal for the manufacture of many objects including axes, knives, chisels, hammers, saws and jewellery.

The Iron Age probably started in Asia Minor around 1500 BCE. Pure iron has a melting point of 1540° C, a temperature that could not be obtained that early. Early wrought iron was produced in the solid state by the chemical reduction of iron ore to

Fig. 7.1 Traditional furnace constructed by smelters from the Haya tribe in Tanzania. The temperature in such a furnace can reach 1800° C. Furnaces extremely similar to this one are known from Early Iron Age sites by Lake Victoria.

iron at about 1200° C with the aid of charcoal. If the ratio of fuel to ore is large, and the bellows are effective, the iron can be made to absorb so much carbon that it forms the alloy of iron and carbon known as 'cast iron'. This melts at 1150° C.

Although iron is more difficult to obtain from iron ore than bronze is to make, it has various advantages. Iron is harder than bronze and can be made to give a sharper edge. Iron ore is also very abundant, so that once the technology had been developed, iron became relatively cheap.

Africa became a major centre for the iron industry during the early Iron Age. The Bantu in what we now call Malawi produced large amounts of iron. 'Malawi' means 'land of flames' – the flames coming from the blast furnaces.

The first steel may have been made 2000 years ago in what is now Tanzania. Steel is iron that contains between 0.1 and 0.5 per cent carbon in the form of iron carbide (Fe_3C). In 1976, the anthropologist Peter Schmidt persuaded some elderly smelters from the Haya tribe in Tanzania to construct a traditional furnace (Fig. 7.1). A bowl, some 50 cm deep, is dug and lined with mud from a termite mound. The chimney is made of old, refractory slag and termite mud, and stands 150 cm high. Eight blowpipes are inserted to varying depths at the base of the furnace, and eight bellows are used to force air into the blowpipes. Swamp grass is burned in the bowl to provide a bed for carefully sifted charcoal. The charcoal and iron ore are then added through the top of the furnace and

Fig. 7.2 Flexible vulture collar of gold inlaid with dark-blue, red and green glass, found on the mummy of Tutankhamen. There is a small matching *menkhet*-counterpoise. From the tomb of Tutankhamen, Valley of the Kings, 18th Dynasty (*c.* 1336–1327 BCE).

air blown continuously through the blowpipes for seven to eight hours.

Measurements showed that temperatures in the blast zone of the furnace exceeded 1800° C. Subsequent excavations have revealed over a dozen early Iron Age furnaces at Kemondo Bay on the coast of Lake Victoria, one of the most heavily used early Iron Age industrial sites in Africa. These furnaces had physical properties very similar to the reconstructed pit, including evidence of the insertion of blowpipes.

By 300 CE, iron casting in India had advanced to the point where huge pillars could be made. A wrought iron column at Delhi is 7.2 m high, 40 cm in diameter and has a mass of over 6 tonnes. Nothing like it was made in Europe until the nineteenth century. This column has remained rust-free, though how such protection was achieved is unknown.

Many museums have dated artefacts from the Bronze and Iron Ages, not to mention the Stone Age. Museums can tell us a tremendous amount about how and why people used different materials, depending on their physical and chemical properties. The beauty of metal work is particularly apparent in certain jewellery (Fig. 7.2).

Plastics

Lacquer was in use in China by at least the thirteenth century BCE. Queen Fu Hao of that time was buried in a lacquered coffin, discovered when her intact tomb was excavated in 1976. Lacquer is a natural plastic. It is obtained by tapping the sap of the lacquer tree (*Rhus verniciflua*), indigenous to China. Lacquer has remarkable powers of preservation, strength and durability. It is insoluble in most solvents and resistant to decomposition.

Separating and purifying mixtures

Classroom strategies

The very diversity of ways in which mixtures can be separated and purified makes it an ideal topic for a multicultural approach. I remember seeing one very successful lesson where much of the time was spent looking at various objects used for separating things that had been brought in by the 12- and 13-year-olds from home. Such an activity could then lead into a discussion of the principles behind the various approaches to separation and purification. It is worth getting pupils to think about the *reasons* for separating and purifying mixtures:

● Why do people want pure salt?
● What can be got from distillation?
● What use is it that iron can be separated from aluminium because it is attracted by a magnet?
● How can the fact that different substances have different melting points be used to good effect?

Conversely, when is it a nuisance that mixtures separate out? (salad dressings, paints, etc.).

Alchemy

Mary the Jewess (first or second century CE) was an Alexandrian alchemist. She invented or elaborated several pieces of chemical apparatus, among them the three-armed still and a type of water bath. Her still consisted of a main flask in which a mixture of substances was placed. This flask was heated and vapours from it ascended into a copper sphere from which protruded three arms, each nearly a metre long. Each of these led to a glass flask where the condensed vapours collected. Another piece of apparatus she devised was a type of water bath. Her name was given to this device: hence the term *bain-marie*.

The items made by Mary and other alchemists were used for separating substances. It is difficult for us now fully to appreciate what alchemy was. It is true that alchemy gave rise to modern chemistry, but the alchemists would have considered that only a very partial understanding of their efforts. In our language, alchemy combines elements of chemistry, religion, magic and psychology. By the sixth century BCE there were at least two great centres of alchemy: China and Greece. Greek alchemy may have had its roots in the much older alchemical traditions that came from the Egyptians embalmers.

Many alchemists devoted their lives to trying to find a way to make gold from other substances. This was not just because of the commercial value of gold, but because the ability of gold to resist decay meant that it was seen as the key to prolonging human life. Attempts to make gold became attempts to find the 'philosopher's stone' – an object whose presence would allow the transmutation of other metals into gold. The search to make gold and to find the elixir of life were essentially one and the same thing. The fundamental assumption behind much of alchemy is put very well by Bronowski in his *The Ascent of Man*:

> Alchemy is much more than a set of mechanical tricks or a vague belief in sympathetic magic. It is from the outset a theory of how the world is related to human life. In a time when there was no clear distinction between substance and process, element and action, the alchemical elements were also aspects of the human personality – just as the Greek elements were also the four humours which the human temperament combines. . . .
>
> To the alchemists then there was a sympathy between the microcosm of the human body and the macrocosm of nature. A volcano on a grand scale was like a boil; a tempest and rainstorm was like a fit of weeping. Under these superficial analogies lay the deeper concept, which is that the universe and the body are made of the same materials, or principles, or elements.
>
> (Bronowski, 1973: 138)

Many contributions to modern-day chemistry were made by Islamic alchemists. Jābir ibn Ḥayyān (eighth century) had his own laboratory. He left instructions for making white lead (carbonate), sal ammoniac, nitric acid and sulphuric acid and found that a mixture of these two acids, aqua regia, would dissolve gold and silver. He knew that copper produces a green colour in a flame, and how manganese dioxide could be used to colour glass. He also improved the technique of distillation and this was subsequently used in the Islamic perfume industry. Rose water is made by condensing the steam and flower oils that result when rose petals are put in a steam distillation apparatus (a procedure which can easily be repeated under school laboratory conditions).

One of Jabir's disciples, Al-Rāzī, wrote of such chemical techniques as distillation, calcination, crystallization and sublimation, and of such apparatus as beakers, flasks, phials, naphtha lamps, smelting furnaces, shears, alembics, pestles and mortars.

Among the many chemical terms that are derived from Arabic are: alcohol, alkali (from the Arabic for potassium carbonate), arsenic, cinnabar, elixir, Na (the chemical symbol for sodium, from *natrun*, the Arabic for sodium carbonate), naphtha and sugar.

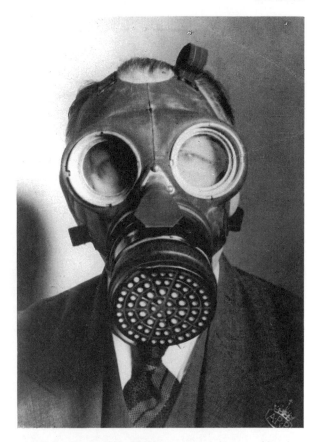

Fig. 7.3 Second World War gas mask invented by the Afro-American Garret Morgan. It is being worn by an A.R.P. (Air Raid Personnel).

Other background information

Brazil leads the world in the technology of making alcohol from sugar and cassava and using it as a fuel for road vehicles. Originally developed as a way of reducing the cost of oil imports, an environmental benefit is that alcohol, on combustion, produces very little except water vapour and carbon dioxide, unlike petrol which also produces oxides of nitrogen and sulphur. The alcohol is produced by standard fractional distillation, hydrated ethyl alcohol being taken off at 78°C. Some vehicles can use this as a fuel on its own. However, most vehicles use a blend of petrol and alcohol and for this anhydrous alcohol is needed, achieved by azeotropic distillation with benzene or hexane.

In 1914, the gas mask used by soldiers and others during the Second World War was invented by the

Afro-American Garret Morgan (Fig. 7.3). A gas mask filters the air. (In 1923, Morgan devised the automatic traffic lights used on roads throughout the world to this day, but was forced, through lack of funds, to sell his patent to GEC.)

Discovery of rhenium

Ida Tacke Noddack was born in 1896 and educated in Berlin. With O. Berg she found element 75 in the mineral columbite. They named the element rhenium after the Rhine. Later, Noddack was the first person to suggest the existence of nuclear fission, as a possible explanation for some experimental results obtained by Fermi. However, she was ahead of her time and her idea was rather passed over. Five years later, though, she was shown to have been correct.

Subatomic particles

Satyendra Bose (1894–1974) was educated in Calcutta and held academic appointments at the Calcutta University College of Science and at the University of Dacca. In 1924 he derived Planck's black body radiation law without having to assume classical electrodynamics. He worked with Einstein and together they derived the Bose–Einstein statistics for use in quantum statistics. Because of this work, bosons are named in his honour.

Maria Goeppert (1906–72), despite much discrimination against her because she was a woman, succeeded in doing important experimental work, though without being paid for it, at Columbia University, USA, before the Second World War. After the War she went to Chicago and in 1948 she found the pattern of 'magic numbers' – 2, 8, 20, 28, 50, 82 and 126. Atomic nuclei with this number of neutrons or protons are particularly stable. By 1950 she had worked out a complete shell model for atomic nuclei which predicted these numbers. For this work she shared a Nobel Prize in 1963 with J. H. D. Jensen of Heidelberg who had arrived independently at much the same theory.

Samuel Chao Chung Ting, though born in 1936 in the USA, was educated in China and Taiwan before working in Geneva and in the USA. In 1974 he, and independently Burton Richter, discovered the new, heavy J/psi particle.

Explanations of the properties of materials

Radioactivity

Marie Curie

Manya Sklodowska was born in 1867 in Poland. After working as a governess, she entered the Sorbonne in Paris as a student in 1891. She lived a most spartan existence, partly because of shortage of money and partly through personal choice, but graduated in physics with a First Class degree in 1893. In 1895 she married Pierre Curie and changed her name from the Polish Manya to the French Marie.

Marie and Pierre Curie jointly carried out research into radioactivity (itself a term coined by Marie Curie). In 1896, Henri Becquerel discovered the radiation-emitting properties of uranium salts. Marie Curie postulated that the capacity to emit radiation was an *atomic* property and showed that the element thorium also emitted radioactivity. She then started to look for further radioactive substances with her husband. The Curies used their savings to purchase pitchblende from which uranium had already been extracted and in 1898 announced the discovery of two new elements – polonium and radium.

In 1903 Marie and Pierre Curie were awarded the Nobel prize for physics jointly with Henri Becquerel. Despite the fame that attached to this, Marie continued to have to teach physics at a girls' high school, in order to help support the family, until 1906. In this year Pierre was killed, knocked down by a horse-drawn wagon while in poor health. Marie was appointed to fill his vacant chair at the Sorbonne – the first woman professor in France.

In 1911 opposition by some of her colleagues led to her being refused election to the French Academy of Sciences, but soon after, in the same year, she was awarded the Nobel Prize for chemistry, thus becoming the first person to be awarded two Nobel Prizes.

Marie Curie was the epitome of a dedicated scientist (Fig. 7.4). The four years it took to purify polonium and radium from pitchblende consisted of four years of continuous hard physical work, often spending day after day stirring the great quantities of material. She and Pierre refused to take advantage of the lucrative industry that grew up around their discovery and isolation of radium, believing that investigators should not profit from the results of their research. During the First World War, she and her daughter, Irene, worked in what became known as 'Little Curies', mobile X-ray cars set up by Marie Curie to take X-rays of soldiers injured by lodged bullets.

Fig. 7.4   Marie Curie at work in her laboratory.

Marie Curie died of leukaemia, presumably the consequences of repeated exposure to radiation, in 1934. In 1935 her daughter, Irene, and son-in-law were themselves awarded the Nobel Prize in chemistry for their discovery of induced or 'artificial' radioactivity. In 1933 the two of them had bombarded aluminium with alpha-particles, giving rise to a novel radioisotope of phosphorus. Since then such novel radioisotopes have been of great value, particularly in medicine.

Lise Meitner

Lise Meitner was a physicist who worked on radioactivity during the first half of this century with a colleague, Otto Hahn. It was known that uranium (atomic number 92) seemed to decay into actinium (atomic number 89). However, enough was understood to realize that this decay was unlikely to happen in one step as radioactive decay only leads to a change in atomic number when an alpha-particle is given off (in which case the atomic number decreases by two) or when a beta-particle is given off (in which case the atomic number increases by one).

Lise Meitner and Otto Hahn suggested that the so-far undiscovered element with an atomic number of 91 might be involved. Uranium could lose an alpha-particle, changing into thorium (atomic number 90); thorium could lose a beta-particle, changing into the undiscovered element (atomic number 91); this in turn could lose an alpha-particle, changing into actinium (atomic number 89).

During the First World War, Otto Hahn was able to do little research, but on 29 December 1917 he got the letter from Lise that he had been hoping for: she had isolated the previously undiscovered element 91. Although Hahn had taken little active part in the work, Lise put his name on the paper in which she reported the result, naming the new element protactinium.

In the late 1930s, Lise's Jewish ancestry meant that she had to leave Germany, fleeing from the Nazis. She went to Sweden, but continued to correspond with Otto Hahn. In 1938 he told her about some puzzling results he and a colleague had come across using a piece of apparatus Lise had helped to design and build. When they bombarded uranium with neutrons, barium was produced (atomic number 56). How could this be? After Hahn had returned to Germany, Lise suddenly realized what was going on: the uranium nucleus had been split in two. Nuclear fission had occurred. She wrote to Hahn telling him this and pointed out that if barium had been formed, krypton (atomic number 36) must have been too, as $92 - 56 = 36$. Hahn looked for krypton and found it, just as Lise had predicted.

However, when Hahn published his results, he omitted Lise's name. In 1944 Otto Hahn, but not Lise Meitner, was awarded the Nobel Prize for the discovery of nuclear fission. Lise Meitner lived on till 1968, but never complained at the injustice done to her. The truth about the discovery of nuclear fission was only subsequently brought to light, partly by her nephew, Otto Frisch, and partly through the research of Ruth Sime, of Sacramento City College, California.

Chemical changes

Combustion and cooking

The archaeological definition of the genus *Homo* is that its members make tools. Although the dating of fossils, particularly those leading to modern day humans, *Homo sapiens*, is not an exact science, *H. habilis* probably existed approximately two million years ago. There is some disputed evidence that *H. habilis* invented fire. Certainly fire was used by *H. erectus* by one million years ago. Hearths dating from this time in the Swartkrans cave in South Africa show the domestic use of fire. Over the last one million years fire has served many purposes. It keeps one warm, scares away predators, provides light, can be used to frighten large prey over cliffs, and is used in cooking. Whether or not knowing how to make a fire requires a knowledge of science depends, of course, on one's definition of science. Certainly, making a fire and cooking require a knowledge of the property of materials.

Fermentation

See use of enzymes and microbes on pp. 66–7.

Firing clay

The first fired ceramics are known from what is now the Czech Republic and Slovakia and date from about 30000 to 25000 BCE. By 9000 BCE, houses made of bricks held together without mortar were being built in Jericho. Around 4000 to 3500 BCE, kilns were in use in Mesopotamia, and within 500 years the potter's wheel was being used there too.

Pupils can make coil pots and fire them outside in their own sawdust-burning kiln. A kiln can be made from ordinary bricks without mortar, surmounted by an iron lid. The chemistry of pigments and glazes can be investigated. For instance, after

a first firing, try soaking a pot in copper sulphate solution or coating in a paste of copper carbonate; then fire again and examine. This can lead into work on flame tests.

Electrolytic reactions – Michael Faraday

See p. 90.

The Earth and its atmosphere

Sedimentary rocks

The Muslim Al-Bīrūnī lived from 973 to about 1051 CE. Among his many writings is the following passage which suggests that he discovered the sedimentary nature of the Ganges Basin:

> But if you have seen the soil of India with your own eyes and meditate on its nature – if you consider the rounded stones found in the earth however deeply you dig, stones that are huge near the mountains and where the rivers have a violent current; stones that are of smaller size at greater distance from the mountains, and where the streams flow more slowly; stones that appear pulverised in the shape of sand where the streams begin to stagnate near their mouths and near the sea – if you consider all this, you could scarcely help thinking that India has once been a sea which by degrees has been filled up by the alluvium of the streams.
>
> (cited by Nasr, 1987: 114)

Al-Bīrūnī went on to write:

> In a similar way, sea has turned into land and land into sea; which changes, if they happened before the existence of man, are not known and if they took place later they are not remembered because with the length of time the record of events breaks off especially if this happens gradually. This only a few can realize.
>
> (cited by Nasr, 1987: 114)

Climatic change

If the Earth had no atmosphere, its average surface temperature would be about $-18°C$. The

Earth's atmosphere acts like a greenhouse, trapping the heat. The natural gases in the atmosphere most responsible for keeping the surface of the Earth relatively warm are carbon dioxide and water vapour. However, as is well known, each year humans are contributing to the greenhouse effect by releasing into the atmosphere huge amounts of carbon dioxide, methane, chlorofluorocarbons, nitrous oxides and other gases. Each year the amount of carbon in the atmosphere increases by about 3×10^{15} g, almost one tonne for each person in the world (Chapman and Reiss, 1992). Per capita the West produces vastly far more than its fair share of these greenhouse gases.

The consequences of all this are still very uncertain. Many climatologists believe that average world surface temperatures have *already* risen by over $0.5°$ C over the last century. There seems to be every chance that the Earth will continue to get warmer. What seems already to have happened is that because of the greenhouse effect, the surface water of the oceans at the equator is hotter than previously. This means that more water from the oceans evaporates into the air. This air then rises faster than usual and causes winds to be stronger. These winds carry the moisture-laden air further from the tropics towards the poles. The result is that sub-tropical latitudes ($5–35°$ N) receive less rain than usual and so are more likely to suffer from droughts.

Another possible consequence of the greenhouse effect is that melting ice is causing sea levels to rise. At the 1992 Earth Summit, leaders of South Pacific island states bitterly criticized the USA for failing to agree to targets for limiting emissions of greenhouse gases, thus risking further rises in sea levels, which may wipe out their lands. A 1992 report issued by the government of the Marshall Islands, and written jointly with American government scientists, concluded that many of the 50 000 islanders would have to be evacuated within a few decades as the sea rises. The government of the Maldives in the Indian Ocean has already had to evacuate four islands for this reason.

Traditional methods of irrigation

More than 1500 years ago the Negev Desert was inhabited by the Nabataeans, desert caravan traders who built such great cities as Petra, Avdat and Shivta. They were able to collect what little rain there was to irrigate their fields. Archaeological excavations have revealed how they managed all this with a rainfall of probably only 10 cm a year. The crucial factor was a highly sophisticated and exhaustive network of stone walls, gulleys and dikes that caught and diverted what little rain did fall. Indeed, long before the Nabataeans lived there, Bedouins did, relying on cisterns carved into the hillsides to provide drinking water for them and their flocks.

Such traditional irrigation techniques are known from all over the world. Recent experiments on the shore of Lake Titicaca have involved the local Quechua Indians redigging ridges using indigenous tools and then planting them with Andean potatoes and grain. The results have been remarkable. Yields have been three times those on the neighbouring fields which use contemporary methods including chemical fertilisers.

All this can be contrasted with the appalling amount of money wasted over the past twenty years on huge irrigation projects sited in developing countries but designed by Western consultants. In 1992 the World Bank admitted that a series of large development projects in the Amazon rain forest, the drought-prone north-east of the country and the slums of São Paulo cost the bank more than $1 billion during the 1970s and 1980s. The projects frequently destroyed the natural environments and led to tens of thousands of poor families being thrown off their land.

Similarly, the Bura Irrigation Project in Kenya, paid for with loans from the World Bank and Britain's Overseas Development Administration, has been a failure. Within four years the project was $100 million over budget and the World Bank pulled out. The scheme created only 40 per cent of the employment intended at treble the cost. Water supply down the project's canal has been unreliable because of pump failure, and crop yields have suffered. Farmers are in debt, charges for the

Fig. 7.5 A modern reconstruction of Chang Heng's seismograph of 132 CE. The original was almost 2 m in diameter. The toad into which a ball fell indicated the direction of the epicentre of the earthquake.

sporadic irrigation water are high and yields are low.

Sadly, these two cases are *not* isolated instances. It is very probably the case that it would have been better if the *majority* of such Western-designed irrigation projects had never started. Whether international organizations will really be prepared to learn from indigenous wisdom and experience remains to be seen.

Earthquake detection

China has always experienced earthquakes. Earthquakes were often the trigger for food riots, or attempts at rebellion. The government had every reason for wanting to know as soon as possible of any earthquakes in distant provinces. In 132 CE, Chang Heng, Astronomer Royal during the later

Han Dynasty, unveiled his seismograph earthquake detector (Fig. 7.5). The signal for an earthquake was the falling of a bronze ball into the open mouth of a bronze toad. At first court officials found it difficult to believe that Chang Heng's seismograph could work. The official historian of the day tells how they were convinced:

> On one occasion one of the dragons let fall a ball from its mouth though no perceptible shock could be felt. All the scholars at the capital were astonished at this strange effect occurring without any evidence of an earthquake to cause it. But several days later a messenger arrived bringing news of an earthquake in Lung-Hsi [about 700 kilometres to the north-west]. Upon this everyone admitted the mysterious power of the instrument.
>
> (cited in Temple, 1991: 163)

CHAPTER 8

Physical processes

In 1894 the eminent physicist Albert A. Michelson stated: 'The more important fundamental laws and facts of physical science have all been discovered, and these are now so firmly established that the possibility of their ever being supplanted in consequence of new discoveries is exceedingly remote . . . Our future discoveries must be looked for in the sixth place of decimals.'

(Drexler, 1990: 152)

Electricity and magnetism

Magnetism, magnetic declination, remanence and induction

Europe acquired the compass from the Chinese. In the book *Dream Pool Essays* published in about 1086, the Chinese scientist Shen Kua wrote:

> Magicians rub the point of a needle with the lodestone; then it is able to point to the south . . . It is best to suspend it by a single cocoon fibre of new silk attached to the centre of the needle by a piece of wax the size of a mustard seed – then, hanging in a windless place, it will always point to the south.

(cited in Temple, 1991: 149)

Exactly when the compass was invented in China is uncertain: it was certainly hundreds of years before Shen Kua lived. A stone relief from the Han Dynasty, dated to 114 CE, shows a compass in use. What may have been a compass dating from 1000 BCE was excavated in Olmerc ruins in 1967 in southern Veracruz, Mexico. The first recorded use of the compass for navigation is from a book called *P'ingchow Table Talk* written by Chu Yü and dating from 1117.

The angle between the geographical North Pole and a compass needle pointing at the magnetic North Pole is known as the angle of declination. By the ninth century CE, it was known to the Chinese.

Europeans do not seem to have known about it until the fifteenth century.

At a temperature known as the Curie temperature – after Pierre Curie – a magnet loses its magnetism (770° C for iron). If the magnet then cools down, it can take on magnetic properties if it lies in a magnetic field. This is the phenomenon of magnetic remanence, acquired through magnetic induction. By the eleventh century CE, the Chinese knew that a piece of cooling iron can take on a slight magnetism from the Earth's field alone, provided the iron is orientated north–south as it cools.

The electric light bulb

Lewis Howard Latimer (1848–1928) was an African-American scientist born six years after his father had escaped from slavery by fleeing from his masters. When Edison invented the electric light bulb in 1879, the bulbs lasted only a week. Latimer's work led to bulbs that could burn for months. He received patents for his inventions in 1881 and 1882 and became the chief designer for the installation of electric lights in Canada, New York and Philadelphia. His company sent him to London to set up an Electric Light Department. In London he met with much racial prejudice. He continued his work in London because of his faith in a just God and a belief that black people should set an example of excellence wherever they found themselves.

Electrochemistry and electromagnetism – Michael Faraday

Michael Faraday was born in 1791. His parents were James Faraday, a blacksmith in a tiny hamlet in a remote valley in Westmorland, and Margaret, a farm servant. At the age of 13 Michael Faraday started work with a bookseller as an errand boy. His employer allowed him to read many of the books that were sent in to be bound, and Faraday developed a keen interest in science.

One book Faraday read at this time, which he praised throughout his life, was Jane Marcet's *Conversations on Chemistry*. Jane Marcet wrote many books on science, and her *Conversations on Chemistry* went through many editions. This was the book that introduced Faraday to electrochemistry. He started to carry out some experiments and in 1812 one of the customers at the booksellers gave him some tickets to attend four lectures by Sir Humphrey Davy at the Royal Institution. A year later Faraday managed to get taken on by Davy as an assistant and within two years was publicly credited by Davy for his work on the Davy lamp, used in mines.

Faraday's career took off. In 1823 he was elected a Fellow of the Royal Society and a year later he became the Director of the Royal Institution laboratory. It is difficult to sum up Faraday's work in only a few paragraphs. Much of his early work was on organic chemistry and electrochemistry. He synthesized the first known chlorocarbons and discovered benzene. Among the terms he introduced were 'ion', 'electrolysis', 'electrode', 'anode', 'cathode' and 'electrolyte'. It was Faraday who discovered the relationship between the amount of electricity passed through a solution containing ions and the amount of matter deposited, given off or lost at the anode and cathode. This work is encapsulated in what is known as the Faraday constant, F, equal to the charge required to liberate one mole of singly-charged ions in electrolysis.

In the early nineteenth century, the relationship between electricity and magnetism was one of the unsolved mysteries of science. It was known that a flow of electric charge could cause a compass needle to deflect. Faraday felt that there should be a matching opposite effect. Eventually he succeeded in demonstrating the phenomenon of electromagnetic induction. He suspended a copper disc between the poles of a permanent magnet. When he rotated the disc he was able to detect a potential difference between the rim and the centre of the disc. He had discovered how electricity could be generated by moving an electric conductor through a magnetic field.

Faraday also showed that a moving magnet could induce an electric current – the principle that allows a dynamo to operate – and devised the first motors and transformer. Faraday's work on induced currents is summed up by his two laws of electromagnetic induction. Faraday was also the first person use to use iron filings to show lines of magnetic force.

Michael Faraday was a very modest and deeply religious man, belonging to a small group of Christians called the Sandemans. He could have made a fortune from his scientific discoveries, but declined on ethical grounds. He started the Friday evening lectures and the Christmas lectures at the Royal Institution, both of which continue to this day. He was offered many honours, but turned most of them down, including the Presidency of the Royal Society and the Chair of Chemistry at London University. He died in 1867.

Energy resources and energy transfer

Energy transfer by conduction, convection, radiation and evaporation

The topic of heat transfer lends itself to a multicultural treatment:

- How can you keep a drink cool?
- Why are homes different shapes in different parts of the world? (This is partly, but not entirely, to do with heat transfer; heat transfer is also connected with the nature of the building materials, the aspect of buildings and their ventilation.)

- What are the different ways in which food can be cooked?
- How do people keep warm or cool?

Different energy resources

All cultures have ways of transferring energy. Pupils could explore such methods which include transferring energy from:

- The Sun to evaporate water and so cool and dry things (e.g. clothes, food).
- Water (water wheels).
- Wind (windmills; sails).
- Organisms (eating animals and plants for food; burning wood, charcoal and fossil fuels for heat or light).
- Beasts of burden for ploughing and transport.
- Gunpowder.
- Slaves.

In addition to the suggestions outlined in Chapter 5 in connection with the teaching of nuclear power, teaching about energy could also:

- Examine the arguments for and against the greater use of renewable energy resources.
- Clarify what is meant by 'saving energy'.
- Look at the role played by women in gathering fuels (e.g. firewood).
- Examine links between energy consumption and pollution.
- Look at disparities between countries in their *per capita* energy consumption and intake (e.g. Fig. 8.1).

Gears

Gears were used in North Africa in about 300 BCE.

Forces and their effects

Levers

The origins of levers are lost in antiquity. The construction of the three Egyptian pyramids of Giza in the fifth millennium BCE involved moving and assembling millions of tonnes of stone using

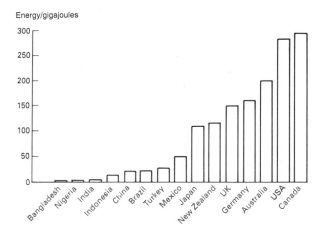

Energy/gigajoules

Fig. 8.1a Annual energy consumption per person in 1987.

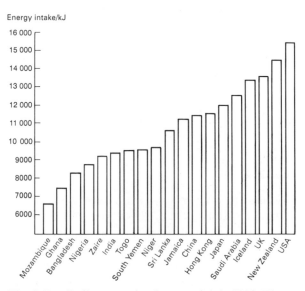

Energy intake/kJ

Fig. 8.1b Daily energy intake per adult in 1990. The World Health Organisation states that the minimum adult daily intake of food should provide 10920 kJ.

ropes, levers, ramps, wedges and rollers. Rollers seem to have given risen to wheels and axles in the Near East in the fourth millennium BCE.

Friction

If we write V for velocity, P for motive power and M for resisting medium, then the Aristotelian view of friction, as contained in Book *IV* of Aristotle's *Physics*, was that $V = P/M$. The Islamic scientist and philosopher Avempace (who died in 1138) believed that $V = P - M$, so that in a vacuum motion would not be instantaneous. This view, known as the Avempace theory, was defended in the Middle Ages by St Thomas and Duns Scotus. It was also known in the Renaissance and is the formula which Galileo gives in his *Pisan Dialogue* against Aristotle's view of motion, without acknowledging its source.

Lubrication

Elijah McCoy was born in 1843, in Ontario, Canada, his parents having run away as slaves in Kentucky. He qualified as a mechanical engineer but because he was black the only job he could get was oiling the moving parts of locomotive engines. In 1872 he patented an automatic system for lubricating engines. This obviated the need for the machine to be stopped before it could be lubricated. So successful was his invention that it gave rise to the phrase 'The real McCoy'. By the time he died in 1929, he held over 50 patents, most of them in the field of automatic lubrication.

Boomerangs

The first boomerangs were made in what is now Poland around 25 000 to 20 000 BCE. Most of what we know about boomerangs comes from Aboriginal tribes in what is now called Australia where boomerangs have been used for many thousands of years. Several different types of boomerang are known. Indeed, not all boomerangs return. Non-returning forms are generally heavier and used to stun or kill prey or enemies. Another non-returning form was used by the Bardi and Nyool Nyool of the Kimberley for fishing in shallow water.

Returning boomerangs in Australia were used to drive birds into nets set across strategic flyways, and in traditional sporting events and games. How they work is difficult to explain in full without an understanding of Bernoulli's theorem and the conservation of angular momentum (see Hess,

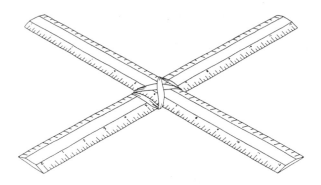

Fig. 8.2   The easiest way to make a boomerang.

1968; Walker, 1985). Careful observation of a returning boomerang shows that it is an aerofoil with a slight twist and characteristic asymmetry. However, there is considerable variety in boomerang shape: even cross-boomerangs are known, made by pegging or lashing two small flat ruler-like pieces of wood at right angles.

It's probably not worth trying to construct a two-armed boomerang in school, unless you want to make the point that they are difficult to make! The easiest type to make is a four-armed one made from two 12-inch (30cm) rulers crossed at right angles and fastened at the centre. The rulers must be the sort that have a flat bottom surface, but an angled or curved upper surface (Fig. 8.2). The two rulers can be attached either by wrapping a strong rubber band tightly around them as shown in Fig. 8.2, or by using a nut and bolt. For safety's sake, never use rulers that have metal edges. This sort of boomerang works equally well for left-handed and right-handed people. The more familiar two-armed boomerangs are nearly always made only for right-handed people.

'Newton's First Law'

Newton's First Law was stated in China in the fourth or third century BCE:

> The cessation of motion is due to the opposing force . . . If there is no opposing force . . . the motion will never stop. This is as true as that an ox is not a horse.

(cited in Temple, 1991: 161)

This quotation is taken from the *Mo Ching*, the collection of writings of a school of philosophers called Mohists after their founder Mo Ti. Their formulation of Newton's First Law was rediscovered by Joseph Needham in 1962.

Nuclear forces

Tsung Dao Lee (born in 1926) studied for his degree in China, though he had to abandon his studies and flee from the Japanese during the Second World War. Chen Ning Yang (born in 1922) received his college education in Kunming in China. Together, in 1956, Lee and Yang showed that the Law of Conservation of Parity (i.e. that physical laws are unaltered in mirror-image systems) does not hold for the weak nuclear interaction. For this Yang and Lee were awarded the Nobel Prize for physics in 1957. They have continued to produce major advances in subatomic physics.

Chien-Shiung Wu (born in 1912) completed her degree in China before moving to the USA. In 1957 she produced the first experimental confirmation of Yang and Lee's prediction about the failure of the Law of Parity to hold for the weak nuclear interaction. Wu has continued to be a major experimental physicist.

Abdus Salam (born in 1926) is a Pakistani theoretical physicist. In 1979 he won the Nobel Prize for physics with Steven Weinberg and Sheldon Glashow. Independently, they worked on the connections between weak nuclear forces and electromagnetic forces. Their work led to the prediction of neutral currents, found at CERN in 1973, and to the prediction of intermediate vector bosons, found in 1983.

Light and sound

Light

Chang Heng (78–139) was a Chinese astronomer and geophysicist who invented the seismograph (see p. 88). He recognized that the source of the Moon's illumination was sunlight and that lunar eclipses were caused by the Earth's shadow falling upon it.

Ibn al-Haitham (*c*. 965–1038) was an Egyptian Islamic scholar. In the West he is generally known as Alhazen. He rejected the accepted belief that light was emitted by the eye, and took the view that light was emitted from self-luminous sources, was reflected and refracted and perceived by the eye. He wrote a book called *The Treasury of Optics*. In this he discussed lenses, plane mirrors, curved mirrors and the workings of the camera obscura (pin-hole camera). He only turned to physics in middle age as he spent much of his early adulthood pretending to be mad. This was to avoid being punished (possibly even put to death) by the Caliph al-Hakim whom he had upset by his failure to devise a new method of controlling the annual flooding of the Nile. Once the Caliph died in 1021, al-Haitham promptly regained his health and started work again.

Al-Haitham had a lathe on which he made curved lenses and mirrors for his experiments. He studied spherical aberration and realized that in a parabolic mirror all the rays are concentrated at one point so that it is the best type of burning mirror. His work on refraction led him to the principle of 'least time' in the determination of the path taken by a light ray. Rainbows interested him and he advanced our understanding of them, though he did not appreciate the role of refraction in the generation of the colours of a rainbow, only reflection. That discovery had to wait until the thirteenth century when it was made by the Persian Islamic scholar Quṭb al-Dīn al-Shīrāzī and his student Kamāl al-Dīn al-Fārsī.

It is difficult to separate the work of these two scholars. Between them, as a result of experimental investigations into the behaviour of light as it passes through a glass container filled with water, they were able to give an explanation of both the primary and the secondary bow – the former requiring one internal reflection, the latter two. This also explains the reversal of the colours in the two bows.

Chandrasekhara Venkata Raman (1888–1970) obtained a First Class Honours degree from the University of Madras, but was unable to start a career as a physicist in India due to the lack of opportunities. Instead he worked in the Indian Civil Service for ten years, continuing his research in his spare time. This work was sufficient to secure him the professorship of physics at the University of Calcutta in 1917. On viewing the blue colour of the Mediterranean in 1921, he concluded that the traditional explanation of the colour in terms of light scattering from suspended particles was inadequate. Raman realized that the scattering of the light is due to the water molecules themselves. Photons of light gain or lose energy as a result of their interaction with the water molecules. When monochromatic light is used, the wavelengths of the scattered light differ from the incident wavelength by constant amounts. This proved to be one of the earliest confirmations of quantum theory. Raman was awarded the Nobel Prize for physics in 1930.

Sound and music

The earliest evidence for the production of music by humans dates from around 20000 BCE from what is now France. Archaeological evidence includes carved bones that appear to be wind and percussion instruments.

Every human society known produces its own music. When men and women sing together, they often sing an octave apart, that is, the frequency of the notes sung by the women is twice that sung by the men. Except that the division of this interval into *eight* notes is a Western cultural tradition. The Chinese divide it into five parts, the Arabs into 17 and the Indians into 22.

The following sorts of activities are suitable for 7–13-year-olds and allow a multicultural dimension to the subject:

● Involve pupils in making a variety of musical sounds using instruments they have constructed, have brought from home, or that are provided for them.
● Experiment with musical instruments and tuning forks to explore the connection between vibrations and sound.
● Demonstrate the involvement of air in the transmission of sound to our ears by putting some sand or peas on top of a drum and then striking a big cymbal next to the drum (but without the two instruments touching). The sand or peas will move.
● Show that sound takes longer to travel than light by watching a starting pistol (or some other object that simultaneously emits light and noise) from about 100 metres.
● Investigate the factors that can affect the frequency of notes. (These factors differ for different musical instruments.)
● Explore the relationship between frequency and pitch, for instance by adjusting the tautness of a stringed instrument.
● Explore the relationship between the amplitude of a wave and the loudness of the sound that results.
● Discuss what is meant by 'staying in tune'.

The Earth's place in the Universe

Measuring time

Background

A marked bone from Ishango in Zaire, dated to somewhere between 9000 and 6500 BCE, shows the probable recording of months and lunar phases. By 4241 BCE the Egyptians had a calendar of 365 days. Each day was divided into 24 hours. Around 3500 BCE, Sumerian people (present-day Iraq) made the first known shadow clocks. They used a moving shadow produced by the Sun to divide the day into hours. Water clocks were used in Egypt around 2000 BCE. The oldest sundial known (Egyptian) dates back to 1500 BCE.

Chongzhi Zu (429–500), the Chinese astronomer and mathematician, measured the length of the year at 365.2429 days by making extensive observations of the lengths of shadows around the winter solstice. The value accepted today is 365.2422 days.

A 24-hour mechanical clock involves getting something, usually a wheel, to turn at the same speed as the Earth. Once this is achieved, the wheel behaves as a mini-Earth, as the hour of the day is nothing more or less than how far the Earth

Fig. 8.3 A 24-hour mechanical clock in Florence Cathedral. Notice that it goes 'anti-clockwise'. XXIV-o'clock was at sunset (*Ave Maria*). The paintings of the four prophets were done by Uccello in 1443.

has turned today (Fig. 8.3). A 12-hour clock is mechanically slightly easier, as the hour hand can move at twice the speed. The mechanical clock was invented in China and first completed in 725 CE. It was built by the Tantric Buddhist monk and mathematician I-Hsing. It was driven by water which caused a wheel the size of a room to describe a single revolution every 24 hours.

Incense timekeepers played an important role in early Chinese and Japanese social and technological history, in addition to their use for time measurement. They were used in temples for religious rites, in agricultural regions for regulating water for irrigation, in palaces, in government offices and in the studies of scholars.

Galileo Galilei (1564–1642) was an Italian who became a Jesuit novice at the age of 14 and then enroled as a medical student. While studying medicine, Galileo noticed that the time taken for a pendulum to complete a swing is independent of the angle through which it travels. This discovery was made by using his pulse to time the swings of a chandelier during church services. Galileo realized that the regular swing of a pendulum could be the basis of an accurate clock.

The concepts of day, month and year are almost universal among cultures, though a month may vary from 28 to 31 days. A week, though, is a less fixed unit of time. Among indigenous tribes today, weeks vary from four to ten days in length, though the one length almost unused is a seven-day week. In classical Greece, months were split into three weeks each of ten days. The Romans had a market week of eight days ending with a day of rest and festivals. Today's near-universal adoption of the seven-day week is Jewish in origin – the God of the Judaeo-Christian scriptures being recorded as having created the universe in six days and then resting on the seventh day, Saturday. Attempts to change the seven-day week in Western society have not been successful. In 1792 the French Revolutionary Convention decreed that a week would last ten days, but this was dropped once Napoleon came to power. In 1929 the government of the then USSR enacted a five-day week, and in 1932 this was changed to a six-day week; but by 1940 the seven-day week had been restored.

Possible teaching strategies

Brainstorm ideas as to how time can be measured. Some of the methods listed below will be suggested by pupils; others may need to be introduced. Other appropriate methods may be suggested by pupils.

- On a sunny day, push a stick into the ground so that it casts a shadow. Every hour mark where the end of the shadow falls. This is a shadow clock.
- Similarly, make portable sundials.
- Make water clocks. Bore a hole in the bottom of a tin and time how long it takes the water to reach a specified height in a container placed beneath the tin.
- Make candle clocks by timing how long it takes a candle to burn down a specified amount.
- Count one's pulse (approximately five pulses every four seconds).

- Make chemical clocks by adding dilute hydro-chloric acid to different concentrations of sodium thiosulphate and timing how long it takes for an ink cross on paper (placed under a glass flask containing the reactants) to seem to disappear due to the formation of a cloudy precipitate of sulphur.
- Make hour glasses using sand to fall through a fine hole.
- Make pendula. The shorter the pendulum, the less time it takes for each swing.
- Investigate radioactive decay, and see how it can be used to date archaeological remains, fossils and rocks.
- Explain how day and night occur by moving a spherical object (the Earth) on its axis a fixed distance from a lamp (the Sun).
- Count tree rings on the stump of a tree (one ring every year).

Other things one can do about time:

- Make time lines: write down one significant thing that has happened in each of the years of one's life so far.
- Research megalithic remains (e.g. Stonehenge).
- Explore cross-curricular links. See whether any pupils have read Jules Verne's *Around the World in Eighty Days*, the climax of which relies on an understanding of the principles of the International Date Line. Time travel, of course, is fundamental to much science-fiction from H. G. Wells' *The Time Machine* onwards. Bertolt Brecht's *Life of Galileo* is significant for being an important piece of literature based on a scientist.
- Explore the concept of time in paintings. Most paintings are snapshots – especially true of those of Hans Holbein (1497–1543), e.g. *The Ambassadors* in the National Gallery, London, painted in 1533, where Holbein records, in the painting, the date (11 April) on a cylindrical dial and the hour (10.30 a.m.) on a polyhedral dial. However, mediaeval religious paintings often show two or more events in the same picture, e.g. the crucifixion, the deposition from the cross and the resurrection. Marchel Duchamp's *Nude*

Descending a Staircase, painted in 1912, antici-pates the use of strobe-photography.
- Introduce the notion of biological time. Biological time passes faster for smaller organisms, being approximately proportional to the quarter power (i.e. the square root of the square root) of an organism's mass. This is why small animals need to feed more often than large animals with similar diets (compare shrews and tigers).
- Introduce pupils and students to the concept of time, as far as we know first explicitly considered by St Augustine, the fifth century Bishop of Hippo in North Africa, who asked the question whether time has ever had a beginning. Physics students can be introduced to the Theory of Relativity through a consideration of the problem of how one determines whether or not two events are simultaneous if they occur in different places.

Astronomy and cosmology

Every culture has its creation stories and under-standing of the stars and other heavenly bodies. Astronomical inscriptions, some of which have still to be deciphered, were being made by the Maya in central America by 8000 BCE. The Baby-lonians were predicting eclipses by 2900 BCE and keeping star catalogues and planetary records by 1750 BCE under Hammurabi. There is still a tremendous amount that we do not know about the history of astronomy and cosmology. What does seem certain is that most of today's world is so polluted by artificial night-time light that we seriously underestimate what was once visible. There is a reliable record from the summer of 364 BCE that the Chinese astronomer Gan Dej ob-served with the naked eye one of the moons of Jupiter (probably Ganymede). This was 2000 years before Galileo's discovery of some of the moons of Jupiter.

Even more remarkable are the observations of the Dogon of Mali who have a detailed knowledge about the Sirius star system which has caused considerable controversy in academic circles. Sirius, the brightest star in the heavens, is, of course, well known to all peoples, but for the

Fig. 8.4   A reconstruction of the Samarqand Observatory built by Ulugh Beg in the fifteenth century CE.

Dogon the most sacred of their 700-year-old traditions revolve not so much around Sirius, but its small and incredibly dense companion star, Sirius B. Despite the fact that today Sirius B is invisible to the naked eye, the Dogon can still accurately draw in the sand its orbit around Sirius. Further, modern science has confirmed the Dogon's assertion that this orbit takes 50 years.

Systematic observations of sunspots by the Chinese probably began in the fourth century BCE. The first certain Chinese observation of a sunspot, recognized as such rather than as a solar eclipse, dates from 165 BCE.

Many observatories were built in the Muslim world from the ninth century. The peak period of the Islamic observatory as a scientific instrument was reached in the fifteenth century when Ulugh Beg built his observatory at Samarqand (Fig. 8.4). Subsequent Western observatories were greatly influenced by it.

Meghnad Saha (1894–1956) was the professor of physics at the University of Calcutta. It was known that the number of absorption lines in the spectra of stars vary greatly, some showing only hydrogen and helium, others showing numerous metals. In 1920 Saha showed that this did not necessarily mean that the stars differed in their compositions. Rather, that at higher temperatures the absorption lines of neutral metal atoms become very weak. This result can be used to calculate stellar temperatures.

Subrahmanyan Chandrasekhar (born in 1910) showed that when a star has exhausted its nuclear fuel, it collapses inwards due to the force of gravity, but that this collapse is eventually halted by the force exerted outwards by the star's highly compressed and ionized gases. He showed that stars above a certain mass are unable, because of this effect, to evolve into white dwarves. This limiting mass is called the Chandrasekhar limit and equals approximately 1.4 solar masses.

Stephen Hawking (born in 1942) has made major advances in theoretical cosmology despite having had a most disabling neuromuscular condition throughout his academic career (discussed further on p. 38). Hawking has worked on the space–time singularity at the beginning of the universe, on black holes and on the quantum theory of gravity. One of his more intelligible, and remarkable, discoveries was made in 1974 when he showed that black holes – despite their name – can emit thermal radiation. A non-zero temperature can therefore be associated with a black hole.

Of all the fields of science to which Western women have contributed, few have benefited more than astronomy. Perhaps this is because much of astronomy requires skills that have traditionally been valued in women – namely precision, care, accuracy and perseverance. The nineteenth century North American astronomer, Maria Mitchell, suggested that women would be more competent astronomical observers than men because 'the perceptive faculties of women . . . are more acute than those of men'. She argued that:

> the training of girls (bad as it is) leads them to develop these faculties. The fine needlework and the embroidery teach them to measure small spaces. The same delicacy of eye and touch is needed to bisect the image of a star by a spider's web, as to pierce delicate muslin with a fine needle. The small fingers too come into play with a better adaptation to delicate micrometer screws
> . . .

(cited in Ogilvie, 1986: 135)

To this we can add that much important astronomical research has been done by people working at home – after the children have gone to bed – with relatively inexpensive equipment.

At any event, the list of women known to have made significant astronomical contributions is huge. Aglaonike, an astronomer of classical Greek times, was subsequently reported by Plutarch as being able precisely to predict the times of future lunar eclipses. Most classical writers considered such ability magic, and Aglaonike is reported to have encouraged such beliefs, being regarded by her contemporaries as a sorceress.

Caroline Herschel (1750–1848) was a German astronomer who came to England with her brother, William, in 1772. William's hobby was astronomy and together they embarked on a systematic survey of the entire night sky, making their own telescope for the project. At first Caroline had little enthusiasm for the survey, but in 1781 William discovered the planet we now know as Uranus and the two of them moved to a new home. Here Caroline became increasingly involved in astronomy. In 1783 she discovered three new nebulae, but it was only when William was away from home that she had the chance to work on her own. It was during such times over the period 1786 to 1797 that she discovered a total of eight comets. In 1787 she was granted an official salary by the King. As Caroline wrote ' . . . the first money I ever in all my lifetime thought myself to be at liberty to spend to my own liking' (cited in Alic, 1986: 129). Caroline continued to work throughout her long life, dying at the age of 97, being buried with a lock of William's hair. She received many international awards and accolades and, with Mary Somerville, a Scottish writer on science, became the first woman to be made an honorary member of the Royal Society.

Williamina Stevens (1857–1911) was born in Scotland but emigrated to the United States shortly after getting married in 1877. Within two years the marriage had broken up and Stevens found work as a maid in the household of Edward Pickering, the director of Harvard College Observatory. Pickering was impressed by her and offered her part-time employment in the Observatory. By 1881 she was a permanent member of the staff and in 1886 started the work for which she is most remembered – the classification of the stars on the basis of their photographed spectra. She classified over 10000 stars in this way and was elected to the Royal Astronomical Society in 1906.

Henrietta Leavitt (1868–1921) devised a new

method for measuring the distance of stars. Before her work only distances of up to about one hundred light-years could be determined, by measurement of stellar parallax. However, while studying Cepheid variable stars, Leavitt found a relationship between their brightness and their period of light variation.

The definitive work leading to a full standardized naming of lunar formations was largely the work of the British astronomer Mary Blagg (1858–1944). Following her death, a lunar crater was named in her honour.

Mary Evershed (1867–1949) was a British astronomer. Perhaps her most important paper was one in 1913 where she maintained that 'other forces are at work on the Sun's surface besides an eruptive force and gravity'. She argued that electric forces act on ionized gases and magnetic forces exist in the vicinity of sun spots.

Margaret Burbidge (born in 1922) is a British astronomer who has worked on the creation of elements in space (nucleosynthesis), on quasars and on galaxies. In 1957 she published a paper with her husband, Geoffrey, William Fowler and Fred Hoyle. They produced a model showing precisely how a star that initially consisted mostly of hydrogen could give rise first to helium, then to carbon and oxygen, then to magnesium, silicon, sulphur, argon and calcium, then to elements such as iron, nickel, chromium and cobalt, and finally to heavier elements such as selenium, bromine, krypton, tellurium, gold and uranium. Margaret Burbidge has been a Professor at the University of California since 1964, and has been Director of the Royal Greenwich Observatory.

Jocelyn Bell (born in 1943) was a 24-year-old PhD student working with Tony Hewish at Cambridge University when they discovered pulsars. In the 1930s, three scientists had all predicted the existence of neutron stars. Such stars would be extraordinarily dense. They might be only a few kilometres in diameter, but have a mass comparable to that of our Sun. They would spin on their axes in seconds or even milliseconds, and have a gravitational force so strong that electrons could only escape at the magnetic poles, giving rise in the process to radio waves. It was these pulses that Bell and Hewish discovered. By now over 500 pulsars are known and Bell is a professor of physics at the Open University.

In September 1992, two hundred astronomers attended a workshop at the Space Telescope Science Institute at Johns Hopkins University in Baltimore on the status of women in astronomy. One intended outcome is to produce a document, to be called the Baltimore Charter, with guidelines on such matters as sexual harassment, the display of pornography in laboratories and inappropriate advances from supervisors and colleagues.

CHAPTER 9

The way forward

She was a great man whose only fault was in being a woman. A woman who translated and explained Newton
. . . in one word, a very great man.

> (Voltaire writing of his collaborator and lover, Emilie du Châtelet, 1706–49 (cited by Alic, 1986: 139))

Judge me for my own merits, or lack of them, but do not look upon me as a mere appendage to this great general or that renowned scholar, this star that shines at the court of France or that famed author. I am in my own right a whole person, responsible to myself alone for all that I am, all that I say, all that I do. It may be that there are metaphysicians and philosophers whose learning is greater than mine, although I have not met them. Yet they are but frail humans, too, and have their faults; so, when I add the sum total of my graces, I confess that I am inferior to no one.

> (Emilie du Châtelet writing of herself (cited by Alic 1986: 147))

I am very conscious that to try, within the compass of one quite short book, to cover the nature of science, the purpose of school science, how to teach controversial issues, what should be in science syllabuses appropriate for a pluralist society, how science should be taught over the 5 to 16 age range to the whole school population, and to provide potted histories of the contributions made particularly by women and black scientists to biology, chemistry and physics may strike some as being a trifle overambitious. In my defence I would argue that is *only* by looking at all this that one can decide what should be learned in school science and how it should be taught. I hope that any readers who accept my argument that there is no such thing as a single acultural science, but rather a collection of ethnosciences, can see how the rest of this book flows from this fundamental premise.

There is much that I would have liked to include, but was not able to through lack of space and my own ignorance. I think that much more could be written about *why* particular scientists reach the conclusions they do. I remember seeing Bronowski's television series *The Ascent of Man* some twenty years ago and recall his suggestion – though

I doubt if it is a correct one – that maybe Mendel got his particulate (rather than blending) theory of inheritance from something that:

> is so obvious that perhaps no scientist would think of it: but a child, or a monk might. That model is sex. Animals have been copulating for millions of years, and males and females of the same species do not produce sexual monsters or hermaphrodites: they produce either a male or a female.
>
> (Bronowski, 1973: 387)

I would have liked, too, to have written more about the domain of science. The mediaeval Muslim authors considered that any particular branch of scientific knowledge could be pursued too far 'such as would be true of a branch of a tree which, by continuing to grow indefinitely, would end by destroying the harmony of the tree as a whole' (Nasr, 1987: 59). Many, but not all, scientists from other traditions would agree. More recently, Nicholas Maxwell (1984) has argued that a radical change is needed in the fundamental intellectual aims and methods of inquiry of science. At present, science has as its end the advancement of *knowledge*. Maxwell argues that this needs to change into a science which has as its fundamental aim the enhancement of personal and social *wisdom*. Further, Maxwell's contention is that such a science would not only be of greater human value than what we have at present, but would be more intellectually rigorous.

One of the things that struck me while I was writing Chapters 6 to 8, was that although the scientists I included were almost all women and non-Western scientists, other categories could have been included. I could have included more scientists who had to struggle to overcome poverty, poor educational backgrounds or other difficult circumstances before they were able to do their scientific work. Examples include:

- Joseph Priestley (1733–1804), the English Unitarian minister who had been orphaned and often ill during a difficult childhood, but who went on to discover the gases we now know as HCl, NO, N_2O, NO_2, NH_3, N_2, CO, SO_2 and O_2, and to show that oxygen is produced by plants and is essential for animals.
- Jean Fabre (1823–1915), the French entomologist who spent most of his working life as a teacher before beginning, in his 50s, the academic work for which he is now remembered.
- Josef Stefan (1835–1893), neither of whose parents could read or write but who became professor of physics at Vienna at the age of 28

and is now chiefly remembered for his work in deriving, with his ex-student, the Stefan-Boltzmann law.

- Clyde Tombaugh (born in 1906), too poor to go to college but who eventually discovered the planet Pluto.

I could have included more scientists who had to overcome persecution, for instance the many Jewish scientists persecuted in Germany during the late 1920s and 1930s. Examples of persecuted Jewish scientists include Richard Willstätter (1872–1942), the organic chemist who worked out the structures of chlorophyll *a* and *b*. Similarly, I could have written about Louis Vauquelin (1763–1829), the French analytical chemist who was forced to leave Paris in 1793 because he rescued a Swiss soldier from a mob during the French Revolution, but who went on to discover chromium and beryllium. I could have written more about how many scientists were influenced by their religious beliefs – it is worth noting that the person who thought up the Big Bang theory for the origin of the universe was Abbé Georges Lemaître (1894–1966), a Roman Catholic priest who was also professor of astronomy at Louvain in Belgium.

Once one thinks about it, most of us belong to a minority group. Science education for a pluralist society is science education for *all*, not for a minority.

References and bibliography

ActionAid (n.d.) *How Many Children?* London, ActionAid. Available from ActionAid, Hamlyn House, Archway, London N19 5PG.

Agyeman, J. (1991) Hardy perennials, *Times Educational Supplement*, 21 June: 43.

Agyeman, J. (1992) Environmental education and global politics, *Humane Education Newsletter*, 3(1): 1–5.

Ainscow, M. (1991) Effective schools for all: an alternative approach to special needs in education, *Cambridge Journal of Education*, 21: 293–308.

Akerman, K. (1990) *Aboriginal Australia Culture and Society: Tools, Weapons and Utensils*. Woden ACT, Aboriginal and Torres Strait Islander Commission.

Al-Faruqi, I. R. and Nasseef, A. O. (eds) (1981) *Social and Natural Sciences: The Islamic Perspective*. King Abdulaziz University, Jeddah, Hodder and Stoughton.

Alic, M. (1986) *Hypatia's Heritage: A History of Women in Science from Antiquity to the Late Nineteenth Century*. London, The Women's Press.

Allcott, T. (n.d.) *Perspectives for Educational Change: An Anti-racist Model and Race and Education in Leicestershire's 'All-white' Schools*. Available from Leicestershire Education Committee, Centre for Multicultural Education, Rushey Mead Centre, Harrison Road, Leicester LE4 6RB. Also available from this address is Leicestershire Education Authority's (1987) *An Aide Mémoire for Multicultural Education: A Checklist of Suggestions for Good Practice*.

Altmant, J. (1980) *Baboon Mothers and Infants*. Cambridge, MA, Harvard University Press.

Amara, J. M. (1987) Indigenous technology of Sierra Leone and the science education of girls, *International Journal of Science Education*, 9: 317–24.

Andrews, C. (1990) *Ancient Egyptian Jewellery*. London, British Museum Publications.

Anishetty, N. M. (1987) *Gene Banks and the World's Food*. Princeton, NJ, Princeton University Press.

Anon (n.d.) *Girls and Science 3*. London, North London Science Centre.

Antonouris, G. (1989) Multicultural science, *School Science Review*, 70(252): 97–100.

Arends, J. and Volman, M. (1992) A comparison of different policies: equal opportunities in education in the Netherlands and the policy of the Inner London Education Authority, *Gender and Education*, 4: 57–66.

Ascher, M. (1991) *Ethnomathematics: A Multicultural View of Mathematical Ideas*. Pacific Grove, CA, Brooks/Cole.

ASE Gender Issues Working Party (1990) *Gender Issues in Science Education*. Hatfield, Association for Science Education.

ASE Language in Science Working Party (1980) *Language in Science*. Hatfield, Association for Science Education.

ASE Multicultural Education Working Party (1990) *Race, Equality and Science Teaching: A Discussion Pack prepared for the 1991 A.S.E. Annual Meeting, University of Birmingham*. Hatfield, Association for Science Education.

Ashrif, S. (1986) Eurocentrism and myopia in science teaching, *Multicultural Teaching*, 5(1): 28–30.

Bain, I. (1984) Will Arno Peters take over the world? *Geographical Magazine*, 56: 342–3.

Baird, V. (1992) Difference and defiance, *The New Internationalist*, 233: 4–7.

Banks, J. (1990) The anti-racist atom, *School Science Review*, 72(259): 150–1.

Barbour, I. G. (1990) *Religion in an Age of Science: The Gifford Lectures 1989–1991, Volume 1*. London, SCM.

Barker, J. A. (1992) Lind and Limeys, part 1: a brief early history of scurvy and the search for its cure in the 18th century, *Journal of Biological Education*, 26: 45–53.

Barnfield, M. *et al.* (1991) *Why on Earth? An Approach to Science with a Global Dimension at Key Stage 2.* Birmingham, Development Education Centre.

Bazin, M. (1987) Tales of underdevelopment, *Race and Class*, 28: 1–12.

Bazler, J. A. and Simonis, D. A. (1991) Are high school chemistry textbooks gender fair?, *Journal of Research in Science Teaching*, 28: 353–62.

Bedini, S. A. (1991) *The Trail of Time: Time Measurement with Incense in East Asia.* Cambridge, Cambridge University Press.

Behrman, N. (1988) *Health in Developing Countries . . . In Perspective.* Cambridge, Hobsons.

Bentley, D. and Watts, D. M. (1986) Courting the positive virtues: a case for feminist science, *European Journal of Science Education*, 8: 121–34.

Bentley, D. and Watts, D. M. (1989) *Learning and Teaching in School Science: Practical Alternatives.* Milton Keynes, Open University Press.

Bernal, M. (1987) *Black Athena: The Afroasiatic Roots of Classical Civilization. Volume I. The Fabrication of Ancient Greece 1785–1985.* London, Free Association Books.

Berry, R. J. (ed.) (1991) *Real Science, Real Faith.* Eastbourne, Monarch.

Best, A. B. (1992) *Teaching Children with Visual Impairments.* Milton Keynes, Open University Press.

Biddlecombe, L., Browne, J., Charlton, B., Dowden, H., Northcott, C., Onslow, J., Priestley, J. and Thompson, J. (1989) *Learning the Hard Way: Women's Oppression in Men's Education.* Houndmills, Basingstoke, Macmillan Education.

Bishop, A. J. (1988) *Mathematical Enculturation: A Cultural Perspective on Mathematics Education.* Dordrecht, Kluwer.

Bishop, A. J. (1990) Western mathematics, the secret weapon of cultural imperialism, *Race and Class*, 32(2): 51–65.

Blackmore, V. and Page, A. (1989) *Evolution: The Great Debate.* Oxford, Lion.

Blaffer Hrdy, S. (1977) *The Langurs of Abu: Female and Male Strategies of Reproduction.* Cambridge, MA, Harvard University Press.

Bourne, J. (1989) *Moving into the Mainstream: LEA Provision for Bilingual Pupils.* Windsor, NFER-Nelson.

Bramwell, D., Hanamann, O., Heywood, V. and Synge, H. (1987) *Botanic Gardens and the World Conservation Strategy.* London, Academic Press.

Brandt, G. L. (1986) *The Realization of Anti-racist Teaching.* London, Falmer.

Brandt, G. L., Turner, S. and Turner, T. (1985) *Science Education in a Multicultural Society: Report on a Conference held at the University of London Institute of Education, Thursday 7 February 1985.* London, University of London Institute of Education.

Bridgeman, K. (n.d.) *Measurement in Focus.* Cambridge, Hobsons.

Bridges, D. (1986) Dealing with controversy in the curriculum: a philosophical perspective, In: *Controversial Issues in the Curriculum*, Wellington, J. J. (ed.), Oxford, Basil Blackwell, pp. 19–38.

Bronowski, J. (1973) *The Ascent of Man.* London, British Broadcasting Corporation.

Brook, A., Driver, R. and Johnston, K. (1989) Learning processes in science: a classroom perspective. In: *Skills and Processes in Science Education: A Critical Analysis*, Wellington, J. (ed.) London, Routledge, pp. 63–82.

Brooke, J. H. (1991) *Science and Religion: Some Historical Perspectives.* Cambridge, Cambridge University Press.

Brophy, M. (1991) Global science, *School Science Review*, 73(262): 59–66.

Brown, C. A. (1990) Girls, boys and technology, *School Science Review*, 71(257): 33–40.

Brown, J. (1991) A journey without answers, *New Scientist*, 8 June: 46–7.

Bryan, J. (1988) *Women History Makers: Health and Science.* London, Macdonald.

Budd, G. (1842) Disorders resulting from defective nutriment, *London Medical Gazette*, 2: 632–6.

Bulman, L. (1985) *Teaching Language and Study Skills in Secondary Science.* London, Heinemann Educational.

Bulmer, R. N. H. (1971) Science, ethnoscience and education, *Papua and New Guinea Journal of Education*, 7(1): 22–33.

Burchell, H. and Millman, V. (eds) (1989) *Changing Perspectives on Gender: New Initiatives in Secondary Education.* Milton Keynes, Open University Press.

Burdet, P. (1985) What have science, education in a multicultural society and all-white schools to do with each other?, *World Studies Journal*, 5(4): 50–6.

Burns, C. J. and Morgan, G. J. D. (n.d.) *Hey! Science is Global!: An Introduction to the History of Science and the Contribution of Black Scientists.* Available from Local Studies Project, c/o The Alumwell Community School, Primley Avenue, Walsall WS2 9UA.

Burns, C. J. and Morgan, G. J. D. (n.d.) *Health: A Real Purpose Project*. Available from Local Studies Project, c/o The Alumwell Community School, Primley Avenue, Walsall WS2 9UA.

Carpenter, K. J. (1986) *The History of Scurvy and Vitamin C*. Cambridge, Cambridge University Press.

Cartwright, R. I. (1987) 'No problem here' – multicultural education in the all white school, *Multicultural Teaching*, 5(2): 10–12.

Cassels, J. R. T. and Johnstone, A. H. (1980) *Understanding of Non-technical Words in Science: A Report of a Research Exercise*. London, Royal Society of Chemistry.

Chalmers, A. (1990) *Science and its Fabrication*. Milton Keynes, Open University Press.

Chamberlain, J. (1992) Oxygen loss threatens Lake Victoria, *New Scientist*, 26 September: 8.

Chamberlain, P. J. (1986) Science education in multicultural Britain, *School Science Review*, 68: 343–8.

Chapman, B. (1991) The overselling of science in the eighties, *School Science Review*, 72(260): 47–63.

Chapman, J. L. (1992) Appendix 1. Recording plant fossils: palaeotaxa or species?, *Review of Palaeobotany and Palynology*, 74: 189–92.

Chapman, J. L. and Reiss, M. J. (1992) *Ecology: Principles and Applications*. Cambridge, Cambridge University Press.

Charlton, D. and Coulter, T. (1990) The Malawi Dam – problem solving in a cross-curricular context, *School Science Review*, 71(256): 142–5.

Charon, J. E. (1989) Contribution of East and West to Spirit–Science Unification, *Muslim Education Quarterly*, 6(3): 45–51.

Cherfas, J. (1992) Farming goes back to its roots, *New Scientist*, 9 May: 12–13.

Chown, M. (1992) What made ripples at the edge of time? *New Scientist*, 15 August: 16.

Clark, S. and Westley, B. (n.d.) *Ordering and Sequencing*. Available from Inter-Cultural Curriculum Support Service, Gorway Block N, Gorway Road, Walsall WS1 3BD.

Clayton, J. (1992) Can they do science?, *New Scientist*, 5 September: 31–4.

Clover, C. (1992) Spotters grouse over name changes, *Daily Telegraph*, 8 August: 1–2.

Clutton-Brock, T. H., Guinness, F. E. and Albon, S. D. (1982) *Red Deer: Behavior and Ecology of Two Sexes*. Chicago, University of Chicago Press.

Cohen, L. and Cohen, A. (eds) (1986) *Multicultural Education: A Sourcebook for Teachers*. Harper and Row, London.

Cole, M. (1989a) 'Whose is this country anyway? Who was here first?': An analysis of the attitudes of white first year BEd students to immigration to Britain, *Multicultural Teaching*, 7(2): 15–17.

Cole, M. (ed.) (1989b) *Education for Equality: Some Guidelines for Good Practice*. London, Routledge.

Collins, H. M. (1985) *Changing Order: Replication and Induction in Scientific Practice*. London, Sage.

Conroy, E. K. and Regan, C. (eds) (1987) *Food Matters: The Question of Food in the World*. Available from Development Education Centre, Selly Oak Colleges, Bristol Road, Birmingham B29 6LE.

Creese, M. R. S. (1991) British women of the nineteenth and early twentieth centuries who contributed to research in the chemical sciences, *British Journal for the History of Science*, 24: 275–305.

Crossley, S. and Marshall, K. (n.d.) *Dinner time!* Available from Bilingual Support Service, c/o Crosby Primary School, Frodingham Road, Scunthorpe DN15 7NL. Also available from the same address are anonymous packs in the same format titled *What's the Weather Today?*, *How does your Garden Grow?* and *Shopping and Food Pack*.

Cunnison, S. and Gurevitch, C. (1990) Implementing a whole school equal opportunities policy: a primary school in Humberside, *Gender and Education*, 2: 283–95.

Dallas, D. (1980) *Teaching Biology Today*. London, Hutchinson.

Darwin, C. (1859) *The Origin of Species by Means of Natural Selection or the Preservation of Favoured Races in the Struggle for Life*. London, John Murray.

Dastagir, H. (1986) A science department's in-service approach, *Multi-Ethnic Education Review*, 5(2): 33–4.

Davis, M. (1991) Multicultural science teaching, *School Science Review*, 72(261): 150.

Davis, S. (1979) *Natural science: natural approach and indigenous content in aboriginal schools*, Developing Education, 7: 20–9.

Davis, S. J. M. (1987) *The Archaeology of Animals*. London, B. T. Batsford.

Dawkins, R. (1986) *The Blind Watchmaker*. Harlow, Longman.

Dayton, L. (1992) Boys hog science and maths classes, *New Scientist*, 18 July: 8.

Dearden, R. F. (1984) *Theory and Practice in Education*. London, Routledge and Kegan Paul.

Deem, R. (ed.) (1984) *Co-education Reconsidered*. Milton Keynes, Open University Press.

Denffer, von, A. (1983) *Ulum Al-Qur'an: An Introduction to the Sciences of the Qur'an*. Islamic Foundation, 223 London Road, Leicester LE2 1ZE.

Dennick, R. (1992a) Analysing multicultural and anti-racist science education, *School Science Review*, 73(264): 79–88.

Dennick, R. (1992b) Opportunities for multicultural and anti-racist perspectives in the Science National Curriculum, *School Science Review*, 73(264): 123–8.

Department of Education and Science and the Welsh Office (1991) *Science in the National Curriculum*. London, HMSO.

Ditchfield, C. (ed.) (1987a) *Better Science. Curriculum Guide 7: Working for a Multicultural Society*. London, Heinemann Educational Books/Hatfield, Association for Science Education, for the School Curriculum Development Committee.

Ditchfield, C. (ed.) (1987b) *Better Science: For Young People with Special Educational Needs – Curriculum Guidance 8*. London, Heinemann Educational Books/Hatfield, Association for Science Education, for the School Curriculum Development Committee.

Ditchfield, C. and Scott, L. (1987) *Better Science: For both Girls and Boys – Curriculum Guide 6*. London, Heinemann Educational Books/Hatfield, Association for Science Education, for the School Curriculum Development Committee.

Donne, B. (1992) Unwelcome visitors, *Natural World*, Autumn: 50.

Drexler, K. E. (1990) *Engines of Creation*. New York, Anchor Books.

Driver, R. (1983) *The Pupil as Scientist?* Milton Keynes, Open University Press.

Driver, R., Guesne, E. and Tiberghien, A. (eds) (1985) *Children's Ideas in Science*. Milton Keynes, Open University Press.

Duyilemi, B. O. (1986) Food plants of Nigeria, *Journal of Biological Education*, 20: 13–14.

Ellis, P. (1992) *Science Changes!* Hemel Hempstead, Simon and Schuster.

Emsley, J. (n.d.) *The Human Element*. London, BBC Education.

Eysenck, H. J. and Kamin, L. (1981) *Intelligence: The Battle for the Mind*. London, Pan.

Fagan, B. M. (1991) *Kingdoms of Gold, Kingdoms of Jade: The Americas before Columbus*. London, Thames and Hudson.

Fagg, S., Skelton, S., Aherne, P. and Thornber, A. (1990) *Science for All*. London, David Fulton.

Fairley, P. (1992) Probably the oldest lager in the world . . ., *New Scientist*, 16 May: 6.

Fathman, A. K. and Quinn, M. E. (1989) *Science for Language Learners*. Englewood Cliffs, N.J., Prentice Hall Regents.

Fensham, P. (1986) Lessons from science education in Thailand: a case study of gender and learning in the physical sciences, *Research in Science Education*, 16: 92–100.

Fensham, P. J. (1988) Familiar but different: some dilemmas and new directions in science education. In: *Developments and Dilemmas in Science Education*, Fensham, P. (ed.), London, Falmer, pp. 1–26.

Feyerabend, P. (1988) *Against Method* (rev. edn.), London, Verso.

Fischer, H. (1864) Klinisches und Experimentalles zur Lehre der Trepanation. *Arch. klin. Chir.*, 6: 595–647.

Foley, D. E. (1991) Reconsidering anthropological explanations of ethnic school failure, *Anthropology and Education Quarterly*, 22: 60–86.

Frazer, M. J. and Kornhauser, A. (eds) (1986) *Ethics and Social Responsibility in Science Education*. Oxford, Pergamon Press.

Freudenthal, G. (1986) *Atom and Individual in the Age of Newton*. Dordrecht, Reidel.

Gardner, P. L. (1978) Difficulties with illative connectives in science amongst secondary school students, *Australian Science Teachers Journal*, 24(3): 23–30.

Gardner, P. L. (1980) The identification of specific difficulties with logical connectives in science among secondary school students, *Journal of Research in Science Teaching*, 17(3): 223–9.

George, J. and Glasgow, J. (1989) Some cultural implications of teaching towards common syllabi in science: a case study from the Caribbean, *School Science Review*, 71(254): 115–23.

Gill, D. and Levidow, L. (eds) (1987) *Anti-racist Science Teaching*. London, Free Association Books.

Gill, D., Mayor, B. and Blair, M. (eds) (1992) *Racism and Education: Structures and Strategies*. London, Sage.

Gill, D., Singh, E. and Vance, M. (1987) Multicultural versus anti-racist science: biology. In: *Anti-racist Science Teaching*, Gill, D. and Levidow, L. (eds), London, Free Association Books, pp. 124–35.

Glick, L. B. (1964) Categories and relations in Gimi natural science, *American Anthropologist*, 66(4) Special Issue: 273–80.

Glynne-Jones, M. (1993) Music: respect for persons, respect for cultures. In: *The Multicultural Dimension of the National Curriculum*, King, A. S. and Reiss, M. J. (eds), London, Falmer, pp. 128–44.

Goodall, J. (1986) *The Chimpanzees of Gombe: Patterns*

of Behavior. Cambridge, MA, Belknap Press of Harvard University Press.

Goonatilake, S. (1984) *Aborted Discovery: Science and Creativity in the Third World*. London, Zed.

Gosling, D. and Musschenga, B. (eds.) (1985) *Science Education and Ethical Values: Introducing Ethics and Religion into the Science Classroom and Laboratory*. Geneva, World Council of Churches and Washington, Georgetown University Press.

Goudsmit, S. A., Claiborne, R. and the Editors of *Life* (1967) *Time*. Time-Life International.

Gould, S. J. (1981) *The Mismeasure of Man*. Harmondsworth, Penguin.

Gowaty, P. A. (1991) [Book review] *Animal Behaviour*, 42: 166–8.

Griffin, C. (n.d.) *Sink or Swim – A Play*. Available from ActionAid (GCSE Resources Clerk), The Old Church House, Church Steps, Frome, Somerset BA11 1PL.

Grinter, R. (1989) Anti-racist strategies in the National Curriculum, *Multicultural Teaching*, 7(3): 34–8.

Hamilton, J. (ed.) (1991) *They Made Our World: Five Centuries of Great Scientists and Inventors*. London, Broadside Books.

Hampshire County Council Education Department (1988) *Education for a Multicultural Society*. Available from The Castle, Winchester SO23 8UG.

Haraway, D. (1989) *Primate Visions: Gender, Race and Nature in the World of Modern Science*. Routledge, Chapman and Hall.

Harding, S. (1991) *Whose Science? Whose Knowledge? Thinking from Women's Lives*. Milton Keynes, Open University Press.

Harris, P. (1991) *Mathematics in a Cultural Context: Aboriginal Perspectives on Space, Time and Money*. Deakin, Victoria, Deakin University.

Hatcher, R. (n.d.) *Magnets: A Second Stage ESL Workbook and Writing in Science and Other Subject Areas*. Available form Inter-Cultural Curriculum Support Service, Gorway Block N, Gorway Road, Walsall WS1 3BD.

Hawkes, N. (1981) *Nuclear*. London, Franklin Watts.

Hawking, S. W. (1988) *A Brief History of Time from the Big Bang to Black Holes*. London, Bantam Press.

Hayes, J. R. (ed.) (1983) *The Genius of Arab Civilization: Source of Renaissance* (2nd edn.), London, Eurabia.

Hazlewood, P. (1985a) Developments in teaching chemistry with a World Studies perspective, *World Studies Journal*, 5(4): 44–6.

Hazlewood, P. (1985b) Chemistry with a World Studies perspective: lesson 'pen-portraits', *World Studies Journal*, 5(4): 47–9.

Hazlewood, P. and Yeo, G. (1985) More about third year chemistry with a World Studies perspective, *School Science Review*, 66: 539–43.

Head, J. (1985) *The Personal Response to Science*. Cambridge, Cambridge University Press.

Heinze, T. F. (1973) *Creation vs. Evolution* (2nd edn.), London, Pickering and Inglis.

Hellemans, A. and Bunch, B. (1989) *The Timetables of Science: A Chronology of the Most Important People and Events in the History of Science*. London, Sidgwick and Jackson.

Hess, F. (1968) The aerodynamics of boomerangs, *Scientific American*, 219(5): 124–36.

Hewson, M. G. A'B. (1988) The ecological context of knowledge: implications for learning science in developing countries, *Journal of Curriculum Studies*, 20: 317–26.

Hiatt, L. R. and Jones, R. (1988) Aboriginal conceptions of the workings of nature. In: *Australian Science in the Making*, Home, R. W. (ed.), Cambridge, Cambridge University Press, pp. 1–22.

Hodson, D. (1990) Democratization, abdication or regulation? Changing patterns of science curriculum development and educational administration in New Zealand since 1960. In: *Case Studies in Curriculum Administration History*, Haft, H. and Hopmann, S. (eds), London, Falmer, pp. 101–24.

Hollingbery, M. (n.d.) *Charles Richard Drew and Elijah McCoy*. Available from Centre for Multicultural Education, Harrison Road, Leicester LE4 6RB.

Hollins, M. (1986) *Girls and Science. Books 1 and 2* (2nd edn.), London, North London Science Centre.

Hoyle, P. (1986) Language and anti-racist science, *Multi-Ethnic Education Review*, 5(1): 33–6.

Hughes, N. F. (1989) *Fossils as Information: New Recording and Stratal Correlation Techniques*. Cambridge, Cambridge University Press.

Hyndman, D. C. (1984) Hunting and the classification of game animals among the Wopkaimin, *Oceania*, 54: 289–309.

Ingle, R. B. and Turner, A. D. (1981) Science curricula as cultural misfits, *European Journal of Science Education*, 3: 357–71.

Inner London Education Authority (n.d.) *Working with Bilingual Beginners in the Secondary School: Science*. Available from Teacher-in-charge, Griffin Manor Language Centre, Plumstead High Street, London SE18 1SL.

Institute of Biology (1989) *Biological Nomenclature:*

Recommendations on Terms, Units and Symbols. London, Institute of Biology.

Jarvis, H. (1992) *We Are What We Eat! But Who Controls Our Choice? An active learning project on food and nutrition with activities for Key Stages 1, 2, 3 and 4* (2nd edn.), London, UNICEF-UK.

Jegede, O. J. and Okebukola, P. A. (1991) The relationship between African traditional cosmology and students' acquisition of a science process skill, *International Journal of Science Education*, 13: 37–47.

Jenkins, E. W. (1992) School science education: towards a reconstruction, *Journal of Curriculum Studies*, 24: 229–46.

Jennison, B. M. and Reiss, M. J. (1991) Does anyone know what energy is?, *Journal of Biological Education*, 25: 173–6.

Johnston, I. (1989) *Measured Tones: The Interplay of Physics and Music*. Bristol, Adam Hilger.

Jones, A. and Butcher, C. (eds) (1990) *Science Education for Teachers of Pupils with Special Educational Needs*. Nottingham Department of Chemistry and Physics, Nottingham Polytechnic.

Jones, A. and Purnell, R. (1992a) *SPECIALS! Science: The Material World*. Dunstable, Bedfordshire, Folens.

Jones, A. and Purnell, R. (1992b) *SPECIALS! Science: The Physical World*. Dunstable, Bedfordshire, Folens.

Jones, G. (1992) When stardom beckoned, *New Scientist*, 18 July: 36–9.

Jones, L. (n.d.) *Science and the Seeds of History* (2nd rev.) Available from 134 Egerton Road South, Chorlton Cum Hardy, Manchester M21 1XJ.

Jones, R. H. (1986) *Science and Mysticism: A Comparative Study of Western Natural Science, Theravada Buddhism, and Advaita Vedanta*. Lewisburg, Bucknell University Press.

Joseph, G. G. (1992) *The Crest of the Peacock*. London, Penguin.

Khan, N. (1991/92) Bilingualism and science teaching, *Multicultural Education Review*, 13: 20–2.

Keller, E. F. (1985) *Reflections on Gender and Science*. New Haven, CN, Yale University Press.

Kelly, A. (ed.) (1987) *Science for Girls*. Milton Keynes, Open University Press.

Kelly, A., Baldry, A., Bolton, E., Edwards, S., Emery, J., Levin, C., Smith, S. and Wills, M. (1985) Traditionalists and trendies: teachers' attitudes to educational issues, *British Educational Research Journal*, 11: 91–104.

Kent, G. (1990) *Practical Guides – Science: Teaching within the National Curriculum*. Leamington Spa, Scholastic.

Kerr, A. (1982) *General Science for Language Learners: A Book for Teachers*. Lancashire Education Committee. Available from Minority Ethnic Groups Support Service, 103 Preston New Road, Blackburn BB2 6BJ.

King, A. S. and Reiss, M. J. (eds) (1993) *The Multicultural Dimension of the National Curriculum*. London, Falmer.

Kirkup, G. and Keller, L. S. (eds) (1992) *Inventing Women: Science, Technology and Gender*. Cambridge, Polity Press.

Klainin, S. (1985) Activity-based Learning in Chemistry. PhD thesis. Victoria, Monash University.

Kysel, F. (1988) Ethnic background and examination results, *Educational Research*, 30: 83–9.

Lambeth Language Centre (n.d.) *Being Scientific, Science – N. C. Ideas, Measurement, Growth and Development, Time and Exploration*. Available from Lambeth Language Centre, Effra School, Effra Parade, London SW2 1PL.

Latour, B. (1987) *Science in Action: How to Follow Scientists and Engineers through Society*. Milton Keynes, Open University Press.

Lawick-Goodall, van, J. (1971) *In the Shadow of Man*. Glasgow, Collins.

Layton, D. (1991) Science education and praxis: the relationship of school science to practical action, *Studies in Science Education*, 19: 43–79.

Layton, D., Davey, A. and Jenkins, E. (1986) Science for Special Social Purposes (SSSP): perspectives on adult scientific literacy, *Studies in Science Education*, 13: 27–52.

Leeds City Council Department of Education (1991) *Gender Equality: A Reality in Schools*. Leeds, Leeds Education Authority.

Leicester, M. (1991) *Equal Opportunities in School: Social Class, Sexuality, Race, Gender and Special Needs*. Harlow, Longman.

Levi, P. (1986) *The Periodic Table*. London, Abacus.

Levidow, L. (ed.) (1986) *Radical Science Essays*. London, Free Association Books.

Levidow, L. (1988) Non-western science, past and present, *Science as Culture*, 3: 101–17.

Levine, J. (ed.) (1990) *Bilingual Learners and the Mainstream Curriculum: Integrated Approaches to Learning and the Teaching and Learning of English as a Second Language in Mainstream Classrooms*. London, Falmer.

Li, S. K. and Owens, D. H. (1978) Sexual selection in

the three-spined stickleback, I. Normative observations, *Zeitschrift für Tierpsychologie*, 46: 359–71.

Lindsay, L. (1985) *Racism, Science Education and the Politics of Food*. All London Teachers Against Racism and Facism Occasional Paper No. 1. Available from ALTARF, Room 216, Panther House, 38 Mount Pleasant, London WC1 0AP.

Longino, H. E. (1990) *Science as Social Knowledge: Values and Objectivity in Scientific Inquiry*. Princeton, N.J., Princeton University Press.

Love, R. M. and Wild, B. (1989) A case study on the relative performance of girls and boys in chemistry, *School Science Review*, 70(252): 112–16.

Luria, A. R. (1976) *Cognitive Development: Its Cultural and Social Foundations* [translated by Lopez-Morillas, M. and Solotaroff, L.]. Cambridge, MA, Harvard University Press.

McDonald, A. and Crossley, R. (1982) *Annie's Coming Out*. London, Penguin.

McInnis, O. (1988) Food – an anti-racist science approach, *Multicultural Curriculum Support Group Newsletter*, 4: 10–13.

McLean, B. and Young, J. (1988) *Multicultural Antiracist Education: A Manual for Primary Schools*. Harlow, Longman.

Maitland, S. (1989) *Multicultural Inset: A Practical Handbook for Teachers*. Nottingham, Stoke on Trent for the Mobile Unit for Development Issues (MUNDI), Trentham Books.

Majno, G. (1991) *The Healing Hand: Man and Wound in the Ancient World*. Cambridge, MA, Harvard University Press.

Mann, A. L. and Vivian, A. C. (1963) *Famous Biologists*. London, Museum Press.

Manning, K. R. (1983) *Black Apollo of Science: The Life of Ernest Everest Just*. Oxford, Oxford University Press.

Marks, J. (1983) *Science and the Making of the Modern World*. Oxford, Heinemann Educational.

Matthews, B. (1989) Chaining the brain: structural discrimination in testing. In: *The Social Contexts of Schooling*, Cole, M. (ed.), London, Falmer, pp. 196–213.

Maxwell, N. (1984) *From Knowledge to Wisdom: A Revolution in the Aims and Methods of Science*. Oxford, Basil Blackwell.

Mayr, E. (1988) *Towards a New Philosophy of Biology: Observations of an Evolutionist*. Cambridge, MA, Belknap Press of Harvard University Press.

Midgley, M. (1992) Can science save its soul? *New Scientist*, 1 August: 24–7.

Millar, D., Millar, I., Millar, J. and Millar, M. (1989) *Chambers' Concise Dictionary of Scientists*. Cambridge, Chambers.

Mitchell, G. (1988) Food – again?, *Multicultural Curriculum Support Group Newsletter*, 4: 2–5.

Mohapatra, J. K. (1991) The interaction of cultural rituals and the concepts of science in student learning: a case study on solar eclipse, *International Journal of Science Education*, 13: 431–7.

Monk, M. (1990) Science and its social context, *School Science Review*, 72(259): 147–8.

Morris, R. (ed.) (1990) *Science Education Worldwide*. Paris, Unesco.

Mowat, F. (1987) *Woman in the Mists: The Story of Dian Fossey and the Mountain Gorillas of Africa*. London, Macdonald.

Mulkey, L. (1987) *Universalism in Science: The Social Organization of Textbook Knowledge*. Unpublished EDRS Report. Available from ERIC (Educational Resources Information Centre), ED 281 770.

Munday, P., Gelbier, S. and Nornoo, D. (1989) Gums – teenagers' perceptions of health, *Health Education Journal*, 48: 85–8.

Murphy, P. (1991) Gender differences in pupils' reactions to practical work. In: *Practical Science: The Role and Reality of Practical Work in School Science*, Woolnough, B. E. (ed.), Milton Keynes, Open University Press, pp. 112–22.

Nasseef, A. O. and Black, P. J. (1984) *Science Education and Religious Values*. Cambridge, Islamic Academy.

Nasr, S. H. (1976) *Islamic Science: An Illustrated Study*. World of Islam Festival Publishing Company.

Nasr, S. H. (1987) *Science and Civilisation in Islam* (2nd edn.), Islamic Texts Society, 5 Green Street, Cambridge CB2 3JU.

National Union of Teachers (1989) *Anti-racism in Education: Guidelines towards a Whole School Policy*. Available from NUT, Hamilton House, Mabledon Place, London WC1H 9BD.

NCC (1992a) *Curriculum Guidance 9: The National Curriculum and Pupils with Severe Learning Difficulties*. York, National Curriculum Council.

NCC (1992b) *The National Curriculum and Pupils with Severe Learning Difficulties: NCC INSET Resources*. York, National Curriculum Council.

NCC (1992c) *Curriculum Guidance 10: Teaching Science to Pupils with Special Educational Needs*. York, National Curriculum Council.

Needham, R. and Hill, P. (1987) *Children's Learning in Science Project: Teaching Strategies for Developing*

Understanding in Science. Leeds, Centre for Studies in Science and Mathematics Education, Leeds University.

Nellist, J. and Nicholl, B. (eds) (1986) *ASE Science Teachers' Handbook*. London, Hutchinson.

Newton, D. P. (1988) *Making Science Education Relevant*. London, Kogan Page.

Nott, M. and Watts, M. (1987) Towards a multicultural and anti-racist science education policy, *Education in Science*, 121: 37–8.

Ogawa, M. (1986) Towards a new rationale of science education in a non-western society, *European Journal of Science Education*, 8: 113–19.

Ogawa, M. (1989) Beyond the tacit framework of 'science' and 'science education' among science educators, *International Journal of Science Education*, 11: 247–50.

Ogbu, I. (1981) School ethnography: a multilevel approach, *Anthropology and Education Quarterly*, 12: 3–20.

Ogilvie, M. B. (1986) *Women in Science: Antiquity through the Nineteenth Century – A Biographical Dictionary with Annotated Bibliography*. Cambridge, MA, Massachusetts Institute of Technology Press.

Ollier, C. D., Drover, D. P. and Godelier, M. (1971) Soil knowledge amongst the Baruya of Womenara, New Guinea, *Oceania*, 42: 33–41.

Osborne, J., Black, P., Smith, M. and Meadows, J. (1990) *Primary Space Project Research Report 1990: Light*. Liverpool, Liverpool University Press.

Osborne, R. and Freyberg, P. (1985) *Learning in Science: The Implications of Children's Science*. Birkenhead, Auckland, Heinemann Education.

Outram, D. (1991) Fat, gorillas and misogyny: women's history in science, *British Journal for the History of Science*, 24: 361–7.

Palmer, W. P. (1990) An annotated aboriginal science bibliography, *The Aboriginal Child at School*, 18(5): 34–43.

Peacock, A. (ed.) (1991) *Science in Primary Schools: The Multicultural Dimension*. Basingstoke, Macmillan Education.

Peacocke, A. R. (1979) *Creation and the World of Science: The Bampton Lectures, 1978*. Oxford, Clarendon Press.

Pearce, F. (1991) Ancient lessons from arid lands, *New Scientist*, 7 December: 42–8.

Pearce, F. (1992a) British aid: a hindrance as much as a help, *New Scientist*, 23 May: 12–13.

Pearce, F. (1992b) World Bank projects punished the poor, *New Scientist*, 18 July: 5.

Pearson, A. (1990) Multicultural science?, *School Science Review*, 72(258): 151–2.

Pike, G. (1986) *Timber! A Simulation Game for Secondary School Students*. Available from Centre for Global Education, University of York, Heslington, York YO1 5DD.

Pike, G. (1987) *Juvenis: The Wonder Drug. A Simulation Game for Upper Secondary School Students*. Available from Centre for Global Education, University of York, Heslington, York YO1 5DD.

Pike, G. and Selby, D. (1988) *Global Teacher, Global Learner*. London, Hodder and Stoughton.

Polkinghorne, J. (1983) *The Way the World Is: The Christian Perspective of a Scientist*. London, Triangle.

Polkinghorne, J. (1988) *Science and Creation: The Search for Understanding*. London, SPCK.

Poole, I. G. (1991) Science teaching in a multicultural society, *School Science Review*, 73(263): 134–6.

Poole, M. W. (1990a,b) Beliefs and values in science education – a Christian perspective (Part 1), *School Science Review*, 71(256): 25–32; (Part 2), *School Science Review*, 71(257): 67–73.

Poole, M. W. (1990c) *A Guide to Science and Belief*. Oxford, Lion.

Poole, M. W. (In press) *Beliefs and Values in Science Education*. Milton Keynes, Open University Press.

Porter, E. (1988) Alternative perspectives on medicine and health care, *World Studies Journal*, 7(1): 8–11.

Powell, R. R. and Garcia, J. (1985) The portrayal of minorities and women in selected elementary science series, *Journal of Research in Science Teaching*, 22: 519–33.

Pratt, J. (1985) The attitudes of teachers. In: *Girl Friendly Schooling*, Whyte, J., Deem, R., Kant, L. and Cruickshank, M. (eds), London, Methuen, pp. 24–35.

Pugh, S. (1990) Introducing multicultural science teaching to a secondary school, *School Science Review*, 71(256): 131–5.

Pumfrey, P. and Reason, R. (1991) *Specific Learning Difficulties (Dyslexia): Challenges and Responses*. Slough, NFER-Nelson.

Pumphrey, S. (1991) History of science in the National Science Curriculum: a critical review of resources and their aims, *British Journal for the History of Science*, 24: 61–78.

Qadir, C. A. (1988) *Philosophy and Science in the Islamic World*. London, Routledge.

Rahman, A. (1981) *Quranic Sciences*. London, Muslim Schools Trust.

Rainey, M. (1988) Food in community life, *Multicultural Curriculum Support Group Newsletter*, 4: 6–9.

Ramsden, J. M. (1990) All quiet on the gender front?, *School Science Review*, 72(259): 49–55.

Reid, D. J. and Hodson, D. (1987) *Special Needs in Ordinary Schools*. London, Cassell Educational.

Reiss, M. J. (1984) Courtship and reproduction in the three-spined stickleback, *Journal of Biological Education*, 18: 197–200.

Reiss, M. J. (1990) Whither multicultural science?, *Journal of Biological Education*, 24: 1–2.

Reiss, M. J. (1991) Science (?) on stamps, *School Science Review*, 73(263): 139–40.

Reiss, M. J. (1992) How should science teachers teach the relationship between science and religion?, *School Science Review*, 74(267): 126–30.

Reiss, M. J. (1993) Science. In: *The Multicultural Dimension of the National Curriculum*, King, A. S and Reiss, M. J. (eds), London, Falmer, pp. 63–77.

Reiss, M. J. (In press) What are the aims of school sex education?, *Cambridge Journal of Education*.

Richie, S. M. (1987) Improving the learning environment for aboriginal students in science classrooms, *Research in Science Education*, 17: 23–30.

Ridley, M. and Rechten, C. (1981) Female sticklebacks prefer to spawn with males whose nests contain eggs, *Behaviour*, 76: 152–61.

Roach, T., Smith, D. and Vazquez, M. (1990) *Bilingual Pupils and Secondary Science*. Available from Schools' Language Centre, Secondary CLSS Team, Smallberry Green, London Road, Isleworth, Middlesex TW7 5AR.

Robitaille, D. and Dirks, M. (1982) Models for the mathematics curriculum, *For the Learning of Mathematics*, 2(3): 3–21.

Rodgers, W. S. (1989) Childrearing in a multicultural society. In: *Child Abuse and Neglect: Facing the Challenge*, Rodgers, W. S., Hevey, D. and Ash E. (eds), B. T. Batsford in association with the Open University.

Rodgers-Jenkinson, F. A. (1990) Multicultural Education and the National Curriculum: An Exploration of Curriculum Policy-Making with Particular Reference to the Study of Geography and History. MPhil thesis, University of Cambridge.

Ronan, C. A. (1983) *The Cambridge Illustrated History of the World's Science*. Cambridge, Cambridge University Press.

Rose, S., Lewontin, R. C. and Kamin, L. J. (1984) *Not in Our Genes: Biology, Ideology and Human Nature*. London, Pantheon Books.

Ross, A. (1986) *Getting Better* [Teaching Pack]. Available from Young Save the Children, Save the Children Fund, Mary Datchelor House, 17 Grove Lane, Camberwell, London SE5 8RD.

Rowland, W. J. (1982) The effects of male nuptial coloration on stickleback aggression: a reexamination, *Behaviour*, 80: 118–26.

Russell, N. (1988) Teaching biology in the wider context: the history of the disciplines as a method 2: worked examples, *Journal of Biological Education*, 22: 129–35.

Russell, T. and Watt, D. (1990) *Primary Space Project Research Report January 1990: Growth*. Liverpool, Liverpool University Press.

Salam, A. (1990) Science, technology and science education in the South, *International Newsletter on Physics Education*, 21 (September).

Samuel, J. (1983a) Mathematics and science – introduction. In: *Sexism in the Secondary Curriculum*, Whyld, J. (ed.), London, Harper and Row, pp. 111–26.

Samuel, J. (1983b) Science. In: *Sexism in the Secondary Curriculum*, Whyld, J. (ed.), London, Harper and Row, pp. 137–47.

Sang, D. (1990) *Nuclear Physics*. Houndmills, Basingstoke, Macmillan Education.

Sardar, Z. (1989) *Explorations in Islamic Science*. London, Mansell.

Sayre, A. (1975) *Rosalind Franklin and DNA*. New York, W. W. Norton.

Schoon, N. (1992) The barbarians in Britain's back yards, *The Independent on Sunday*, 17 May: 7.

Science for a Multicultural Society Group (1985) *Science Education for a Multicultural Society*. Science Curriculum Review in Leicestershire, Leicestershire Education Authority.

Scott, A. W. (1986) Material culture in traditional aboriginal society: fiction and fact, *The Australian Science Teachers Journal*, 32: 9–18.

Scott, F. (1987) Dreamtime technology, *Gender Equality in Maths and Science*, 1(5): 15–22.

Scott, J. (1986) *Energy Through Time: Schools History Project 13–16*. Oxford, Oxford University Press.

Scott, P., Dyson, T. and Gater, S. (1987) *Children's Learning in Science Project: A Constructivist View of Learning and Teaching in Science*. Leeds, Centre for Studies in Science and Mathematics Education.

Secondary Science Curriculum Review (n.d.) *Multicultural Education Through Science: A Resource and Workshop Pack for Science Teachers*. Secondary Science Curriculum Review East/Central Region. Available from Ms S. Barnes, c/o Cistel, Manchester

Polytechnic, 9A Didsbury Park, Didsbury, Manchester M20 8RR.

Selby, D. (1985) Global perspectives in mathematics and science education: a bibliography, *World Studies Journal*, 5(4): 57–8.

Selkirk, D. R. and Burrows, F. J. (eds) (1987) *Confronting Creationism: Defending Darwin*. Kensington, New South Wales, New South Wales University Press.

Sertima, van, I. (ed.) (1983) *Blacks in Science: Ancient and Modern*. New Brunswick, Transaction Books.

Shaharir bin Mohamad Zain (1991) Malaysian experience in Islamization of science, *Muslim Education Quarterly*, 8(2): 15–23.

Shan, S.-J. and Bailey, P. (1991) *Multiple Factors: Classroom Mathematics for Equality and Justice*. Stoke-on-Trent, Trentham Books.

Shan, S. J. Several booklets produced: *Roots of Famine; Biology: An Antiracist Approach; Energy for Ever? An Antiracist Approach; Antiracist Approaches to Science; Ecology: Consequences of Human Activity; Food, Glorious Food*; and *Science, Mathematics and Technology for Education in a Multicultural Society* (with C. Seal). Available from Faculty of Multicultural Education, Birmingham Education Department, Martineau Education Centre, Balden Road, Harborne B32 2EH.

Shortland, M. and Warwick, A. (1989) *Teaching the History of Science*. Oxford, Basil Blackwell.

Siddons, C. and Spurgin, B. (1990) Beliefs and values in science education, *School Science Review*, 72(259): 145–6.

Simpson, A. (1988) *Whose Gold? Geest and Banana Trade*. Latin American Bureau, London. Available from Latin American Bureau, 1 Amwell Street, London EC1R R1L.

Siraj-Blatchford, J. (1987) Creating an anti-racist ethos, *School Science Review*, 68: 756–8.

Siraj-Blatchford, J. (1989) Multicultural science, *School Science Review*, 71(254): 149–50.

Siraj-Blatchford, J. (1990) What is an anti-racist atom?, *School Science Review*, 71(257): 127–31.

Siraj-Blatchford, J. (1991) Multicultural science, *School Science Review*, 73(263): 136–7.

Smail, B. (1984) *Girl-friendly Science: Avoiding Sex Bias in the Curriculum*. York, Longman.

Smith, C. (1982) Teaching issues of race in secondary schools, *Cambridge Journal of Education*, 12: 115–21.

Smith, D. J. and Tomlinson, S. (1989) *The School Effect: A Study of Multi-Racial Comprehensives*. London, Policy Studies Institute.

Smith, J. R. (1987) *The Speckled Monster: Smallpox in England 1670–1970, with particular reference to Essex*. Chelmsford, Essex Record Office.

Solomon, J. (1989) *The Search for Simple Substances*. Hatfield, Association for Science Education.

Solomon, J. (1990) *Stars and Forces*. Hatfield, Association for Science Education.

Solomon, J. (1991) *Exploring the Nature of Science: Key Stage 3*, Glasgow, Blackie.

Solomon, J. (1992) *What is Science? SATIS 16–19*. Hatfield, Association for Science Education.

Spear, M. G. (1984) The biasing influence of pupil sex in a science marking exercise, *Research in Science and Technological Education*, 2: 55–60.

Stacy, S. (1983) Aboriginal nutrition. In: *The Best of the Science Show*, Williams, R. (ed.), Melbourne, Thomas Nelson, pp. 135–41.

Steel, D. (1992) Astronomers fight sexism, *New Scientist*, 26 September: 8.

Sternberg, R. J. (1990) *Metaphors of Mind: Conceptions of the Nature of Intelligence*. Cambridge, Cambridge University Press.

Stumpe, L. H. *et al.* (1988) *School in the World. Teaching for a Global Perspective: Approaches and Resources for Curriculum Development in Junior Schools*. Liverpool, Merseyside Association for World Development Education, Available from The World Development Studies Centre, St Katherine's College, LIHE, Strand Park Road, Liverpool L16 9JD.

Swift, D. (1988) *Physics for GCSE*. Oxford, Basil Blackwell.

Tasker, M. (1989) *The Teaching and Learning of the History of Technology*. London, The Historical Association.

Taylor, C. (1976) *Sounds of Music*. London, British Broadcasting Corporation.

Temple, R. (1991) *The Genius of China: 3000 Years of Science, Discovery, and Invention*. London, Prion/Multimedia.

Ter Pelkwijk, J. J. and Tinbergen, N. (1937) Eine reizbiologische Analyse einiger Verhaltensweisen von *Gasterosteus aculeatus* L., *Zeitschrift für Tierpsychologie*, 1: 193–204.

Thorp, S. (ed.) (1991) *Race, Equality and Science Teaching: An Active INSET Manual for Teachers and Educators*. Hatfield, Association for Science Education.

Tinbergen, N. (1951) *The Study of Instinct*. Oxford, Oxford University Press.

Tomkins, S. (1984) *The Origins of Mankind*. Cambridge, Cambridge University Press.

Tomkins, S. (1989) *Heredity and Human Diversity*. Cambridge, Cambridge University Press.

Tomkins, S., Reiss, M. J. and Morris, C. (1992) *Biology at Work*. Cambridge, Cambridge University Press.

Troyna, B. (1987) Beyond multiculturalism: towards the enactment of antiracist education in policy provision and pedagogy, *Oxford Review of Education*, 13: 307–20.

Troyna, B. and Hatcher, R. (1992) *Racism in Children's Lives: A Study of Mainly-white Primary Schools*. London, Routledge.

Tunnicliffe, S. D. (1986) Teaching science to children from ethnic minority groups, *School Science Review*, 67: 607–11.

Turner, S. and Turner, T. (1987) Multicultural education in the initial training of Science teachers, *Research in Science and Technological Education*, 5: 25–36.

Turner, S. and Turner, T. (1989a) An international dimension to the teaching of science – opportunities in the National Curriculum?, *Multicultural Teaching*, 8(1): 34–9.

Turner, S. and Turner, T. (1989b) *Science, the National Curriculum and Cultural Diversity: Report of a one day conference held on Wednesday, 15 February, 1989, University of London Institute of Education*. Science Education Department, University of London Institute of Education.

Tylecote, R. F. (1992) *A History of Metallurgy* (2nd edn.), London, The Institute of Materials.

Unesco (1983) *Racism, Science and Pseudo-science: Proceedings of the symposium to examine pseudo-scientific theories invoked to justify racism and racial discrimination, Athens, 30 March to 3 April 1981*. Paris, United Nations Educational, Scientific & Cultural Organization.

Vance, M. (1984a) *Assessment in a Multicultural Society. Biology at 16+: A Discussion Document*. York, Longman.

Vance, M. (1984b) Biology. In: *Curriculum Opportunities in a Multicultural Society*, Craft, A. and Bardell, G. (eds), London, Harper and Row, pp. 147–64.

Verma, G. and Pumfrey, P. (eds) (1988) *Educational Attainments: Issues and Outcomes in Multicultural Education*. London, Falmer.

Versey, J. (1990) Taking action on gender issues in science education, *School Science Review*, 71(256): 9–14.

Vines, G. (1992) The Anning inheritance, *New Scientist*, 26 September: 49–50.

Vlaardingerbroek, B. (1990) Ethnoscience and science teacher training in Papua New Guinea, *Journal of Education for Teaching*, 16: 217–24.

Wagner, D. L. (ed.) (1983) *The Seven Liberal Arts in the Middle Ages*. Bloomington, IN, Indiana University Press.

Walford, G. (1980) Sex bias in physics textbooks, *School Science Review*, 62: 220–7.

Walford, R. (ed.) (1985) *Geographical Education for a Multicultural Society: Report of the Working Party set up by the Geographical Association*. Geographical Association. Available from the Geographical Association, 343 Fulwood Road, Sheffield S10 3BP.

Walker, J. (1985) *Roundabout: The Physics of Rotation in the Everyday World: Readings from 'The Amateur Scientist' in* Scientific American. New York, W. H. Freeman.

Ward, A. (1986) Magician in a white coat, *School Science Review*, 68: 348–50.

Watson, J. D. (1970) *The Double Helix: A Personal Account of the Discovery of the Structure of DNA*. Harmondsworth, Penguin.

Watt, D. and Russell, T. (1990) *Primary Space Project Research Report 1990: Sound*. Liverpool, Liverpool University Press.

Watts, S. (1986) Science education for a multicultural society. In: *Multicultural Education: Towards Good Practice*, Arora, R. K. and Duncan, C. G. (eds), London, Routledge and Kegan Paul, pp. 135–146.

Weart, S. R. and Phillips, M. (eds) (1985) *History of Physics: Readings from Physics Today – Number Two*. New York, American Institute of Physics.

Wellington, J. J. (1986) The nuclear issue in the curriculum and the classroom. In: *Controversial Issues in the Curriculum*, Wellington, J. J. (ed.), Oxford, Basil Blackwell, pp. 149–68.

Wellington, J. (ed.) (1989) *Skills and Processes in Science Education: A Critical Analysis*. London, Routledge.

Westley, B. (n.d.) *Language Across the Curriculum/ Science, Language Across the Curriculum/Science Games, Language Across the Curriculum/Science Apparatus Resource Pack, Science Apparatus Bank: Small, Science Apparatus Bank: Medium and Science Apparatus Bank: Large*. Available from Inter-Cultural Curriculum Support Service, Gorway Block N, Gorway Road, Walsall WS1 3BD.

Whitby, V. and Keel, P. (1988) Equality in primary science materials, *Multicultural Teaching*, 7(3): 39.

White, A. J. M. (1978) *What About Origins?* Newton Abbott, Dunestone Printers.

White, M. and Gribbin, J. (1992) *Stephen Hawking: A Life in Science*. London, Viking.

White, J. and Welford, G. (1988) *The Language of Science*. London, Assessment of Performance Unit, Department of Education and Science.

White, R. T. (1988) *Learning Science*. Oxford, Basil Blackwell.

Whitelegg, L. (1992) Girls in science education: of rice and fruit trees. In: *Inventing Women: Science, Technology and Gender*, Kirkup, G. and Keller, L. S. (eds), Cambridge, Polity Press, pp. 178–87.

Whitrow, G. J. (1989) *Time in History: Views of Time from Prehistory to the Present Day*. Oxford, Oxford University Press.

Whyld, J. (ed.) (1983) *Sexism in the Secondary Curriculum*. London, Harper and Row.

Wilkinson, D. A. (1990) The revival of natural theology in contemporary cosmology, *Science and Christian Belief*, 2: 95–115.

Williams, I. W. (ed.) (1983) *Third World Science: Resource Materials for Science Teachers*. Available from The Centre for World Development Education, Regent's College, Inner Circle, Regent's Park, London NW1 4NS.

Williams, I. W. (1984) Chemistry. In: *Curriculum Opportunities in a Multicultural Society*, Craft, A. and Bardell, G. (eds), London, Harper and Row, pp. 133–46.

Williamson, P. (1991) *The Nature of Science*. Cheltenham, Stanley Thornes.

Woolgar, S. (1988) *Science: The Very Idea*. Chichester, Ellis Horwood.

Woolnough, B. E. (1989) Faith in science?, *School Science Review*, 70(252): 133–7.

Woolnough, B. E. (ed.) (1991) *Practical Science: The Role and Reality of Practical Work in School Science*. Milton Keynes, Open University Press.

Wright, D. (1992) The great world map muddle, *Times Educational Supplement*, 10 April: 40–1.

Wyvill, B. (1991) Classroom ideas for antiracism through science in primary education. In: *Science in Primary Schools: The Multicultural Dimension*, Peacock, A. (ed.), Basingstoke, Macmillan Education, pp. 11–27.

Young, N. (1989) *Nicaragua: Testing the Water – from Village Wells to National Plan*. London, Catholic Institute for International Relations, London, Christian Aid, London, Nicaragua Health Fund and Oxford, Oxfam. Available from Catholic Institute for International Relations, 22 Coleman Fields, London N1 7AF.

Resources

In addition to the books, chapters and articles listed in the references and bibliography on pp. 103–114, I have found the following to be very helpful.

Addresses

Access to Information on Multicultural Education. A clearing house for multicultural and anti-racist educational material. Produces an extensive and useful list of educational resources. Available from AIMER, Bulmershe College of Higher Education, Woodlands Avenue, Earley, Reading RG6 1HY.

Baby Milk Action, 23 St Andrew's Street, Cambridge CB2 3AX. Promotes breast feeding and will provide valuable nutritional information about breast and bottle milk.

Black Cultural Archives, 378 Coldharbour Lane, London SW9.

Black Environment Network, Inner Cities Unit, 26 Bedford Square, London WC1B 3HU.

Centre for Alternative Technology, Machynlleth Powys SY20 9AZ, Wales.

Centre for World Development Education. Produces an extensive annual catalogue listing educational materials available from the centre. Available from CWDE, Regent's College, Inner Circle, Regent's Park, London NW1 4NS.

Early Years Trainers Anti-racist Network, 1 The Lyndens, 51 Granville Road, London N12 0JH.

Equal Opportunities Commission, Overseas House, Quay Street, Manchester M3 3HN.

National Maritime Museum. Has a Time Galley which opened in 1992. Details available from National Maritime Museum, Greenwich, London SE10 9NF.

Oxfam. Produce a large number of resources. They will loan photographs (over 10 000 B&W available), slides (20 000), slide sets, slide/tape sets, videos and audio cassettes free of charge. Details available from Oxfam House, 274 Banbury Road, Oxford OX2 7DZ.

Population Crisis Committee, 1120 19th Street N.W., Suite 550, Washington, D.C. 20036, USA. Produces, inter alia, The International Human Suffering Index – a poster that statistically rates living conditions in 141 countries. Each individual country's index is compiled by adding ten measures of human welfare related to such things as life expectancy, access to clean drinking water, secondary school enrollment, infant immunization and political freedom.

Women into Science and Engineering, The Engineering Council, 10 Maltravers Street, London WC2R 3ER. Produces mobile teaching and exhibition centres to tour secondary schools and provide practical experience of technology to help girls develop greater confidence in such areas. Also produces booklets and posters, gives grants, organizes competitions, promotes career breaks for women and arranges courses and visits.

Women's Environmental Network, Aberdeen Studies, 22 Highbury Grove, London N5 2EA.

Education packs and series

Academy of Indian Dance (1992) *Chipko Education Pack*. Contains background information, photographs and other materials for use in science and elsewhere in the curriculum, both at primary and secondary level. Available from Academy of Indian Dance, 16 Flaxman Terrace, London WC1 9AT.

Armitage, P. (1991) *Little Known Contributions to*

Science. OHP masters plus unbound booklet. Available from County of Avon Maths, Science and Technology Centre. Available from MST Centre, Sheridan Road, Horfield, Bristol BS7 0PU.

Development Education Project (1986) A set of seven books titled *Perceptions, Colonialism, Food, Health, Population Changes, Work* and *Aid and Development*. Available from Development Education Project, c/o Manchester Polytechnic, 801 Wilmslow Road, Manchester M20 8RG.

Inner London Education Authority. *The Development Project*. Available from Marketing and Publicity Section, ILEA Learning Resources Branch, Centre for Learning Resources, 275 Kennington Lane, London SE11 5QZ. [A geography project aimed at 13+. Will contain five pupils' books and five teachers' books. Titles include: *What is Development?*, *The Population Puzzle* and *Feeding the World*.]

Computer software

The Water Game: A Topic-based Computer Simulation. 40 track BBC B. Program design by P. Bateson and T. Shepheard; programmed by T. R. S. Wilson; notes by L. Tate; edited by E. Seagall. CWDE Software. Available from The Computer Project, Centre for World Development Education, Regent's College, Inner Circle, Regent's Park, London NW1 4NS.

Book with tape

Mutasa, N. (1991) *Black Scientists and Inventors*, Nottinghamshire Afrikan and Caribbean Education Team. Available from Afrikan and Caribbean Education Team, Glenbrook Management Centre, Wigman Road, Bilborough, Nottingham NG8 4PD.

Jigsaw puzzle

Arno Peters World Map Jigsaw Puzzle: 650 pieces (810 x 525 mm). Available from New Internationalist, 55 Rectory Road, Oxford OX4 1BW.

'Horizon' TV transcripts

In Search of the Noble Savage. Transcript of the programme transmitted 27 January 1992. Available from Horizon: In Search of the Noble Savage, P.O. Box 7, London W3 6XJ.

Iceman. Transcript of the programme transmitted 27 April 1992. Available from Horizon: Iceman, P.O. Box 7, London W3 6XJ.

Teaching pack with 35 mm slides

Gyde, S. (n.d.) *Burundi – Trees for Life*, ActionAid, London. Available from ActionAid, Hemlyn House, Archway, London N19 5PG.

Teaching pack with OHPs

Hayes, P. (ed.) (n.d.) *Marie Curie*. Available from Marie Curie Memorial Foundation, 28 Belgrave Square, London SW1X 8QG.

Wall Chart

North, P. (1991) *The Wall Chart of Discovery and Invention: The growth of human knowledge from prehistory to space travel*, Studio Editions, London. Available from Studio Editions, Princess House, 50 Eastcastle Street, London W1N 7AP.

Video, booklet and posters

Women in Science: Girls and Science Education. Produced by Resources for Learning Ltd on behalf of British Nuclear Fuels plc Education Unit. Available from British Nuclear Fuels plc Education Unit, Risley, Warrington WA3 6AS.

Posters

Achievements in Chemistry: Dorothy Mary Crowfoot Hodgkin and Crystallography. Available from Royal Society of Chemistry, Burlington House, Piccadilly, London W1V 0BN.

Afro-Caribbean Teaching Unit (n.d.) A set of six posters including one of Mary Seacole (nurse) and one of Dr George Washington Carver (scientist). Available from Multicultural Education Faculty, Education Support Service, The Bordesley Centre, Camp Hill, Stratford Road, Birmingham B11 1AR.

Ciba-Geigy (USA) have produced a set of posters titled *Exceptional Black Scientists*, but these are now out of print.

The Equal Opportunities Commission used to have a set of posters titled *Women Scientists* available free, but these are now out of print.

Women into Science and Engineering. Produce posters on women in science and engineering. Available from WISE, The Engineering Council, 10 Maltravers Street, London WC2R 3ER.

Atlas

Akademische Verlagsanstalt, Vaduz (1991) *Compact Peters Atlas of the World*, Longman, Harlow.

Journals

CASTME (Commonwealth Association of Science, Technology and Mathematics Educators) Journal
Gender and Education
International Journal of Science Education
Journal of Education in Museums, 7 (1987) [Whole issue devoted to multicultural education]
Links
Multicultural Education Review
Multicultural Teaching
Muslim Education Quarterly
New Internationalist
Primary Science Review
Race and Class
World Health
World Studies Journal

Index

PRACTICAL SCIENCE
THE ROLE AND REALITY OF PRACTICAL WORK IN SCHOOL SCIENCE

Brian Woolnough (ed.)

Science teaching is essentially a practical activity, with a long tradition of pupil experimental work in schools. And yet, there are still large and fundamental questions about its most appropriate role and the reality of what is actually achieved. What is the purpose of doing practical work? – to increase theoretical understanding or to develop practical competencies? What does it mean to be good at doing science? Do we have a valid model for genuine scientific activity? – and if so do we develop it by teaching the component skills or by giving experience in doing whole investigations? What is the relationship between theoretical understanding and practical performance? How significant is the tacit knowledge of the student, and the scientist, in achieving success in tackling a scientific problem? How important are such factors as motivation and commitment? What do we mean by transferability and progression in respect to practical work? – do they exist? – can they be defined? How can we assess a student's practical ability in a way which is valid and reliable and at the same time encourages, rather than destroys, good scientific practice in schools? This book addresses such questions.

By bringing together the latest insights and research findings from many of the world's leading science educators, new perspectives and guidelines are developed. It provides a re-affirmation of the vital importance of practical activity in science, centred on problem-solving investigations. It advocates the need for students to engage in whole practical tasks, in which all aspects of knowledge (tacit as well as explicit), of practical ability, and of personal attributes of commitment and creativity, are interacting. While considering the particularly pertinent issues arising from the National Curriculum for Science in England, its discussion is equally germane to all concerned with developing good practical work in schools.

Contents
Setting the scene – Practical work in school science: an analysis of current practice – The centrality of practical work in the Science/Technology/Society movement – Practical science in low-income countries – a means to an end: the role of processes in science education – Practical work in science: a task-based approach? – Reconstructing theory from practical experience – Episodes, and the purpose and conduct of practical work – Factors affecting success in science investigations – School laboratory life – Gender differences in pupils' reactions to practical work – Simulation and laboratory practical activity – Tackling technological tasks – Principles of practical assessment – Assessment and evaluation in the science laboratory – Practical science as a holistic activity – References – Index.

Contributors
Terry Allsop, Bob Fairbrother, Geoffrey J. Giddings, Richard Gott, Richard F. Gunstone, Avi Hofstein, Richard Kimbell, Vincent Lunetta, Judith Mashiter, Robin Millar, Patricia Murphy, Joan Solomon, Pinchas Tamir, Kok-Aun Toh, Richard T. White, Brian E. Woolnough, Robert E. Yager.

224pp   0 335 09389 2 (Paperback)   0 335 09390 6 (Hardback)

TEACHING SCIENCE, TECHNOLOGY AND SOCIETY

Joan Solomon

This is the first book to describe an area which has increasingly generated classroom materials, and educational polemic, without any proper discussion of its rationale or aims. Different approaches to the teaching and implementation of STS are used, through the words of teachers, or through descriptions of classroom activity, to explore different facets of its nature. This illuminates the intentions and reality of STS far better than any rigid prescription of its meaning and practice.

Successive chapters describe the history of STS within science and education, its relevance to young children and their families, ways that have been used to introduce it into secondary schools, teaching strategies in the middle school, examinations and modes of assessment, simulations and role-play, and group discussion of values and civic issues.

The book is based on wide personal experience, and makes inspiring and informative reading for practising teachers.

Contents
What and why is STS? – Our youngest pupils – Getting going on STS in the secondary school – Teaching strategies in the secondary school – The examination classes – Games, simulation, and role-play – Group discussion of issues: the DISS Project – References – Index.

80pp   0 335 09952 1 (Paperback)   0 335 09953 X (Hardback)

BIOTECHNOLOGY IN SCHOOLS
A HANDBOOK FOR TEACHERS

Jenny Henderson and Stephen Knutton

In recent years there has been spectacular growth in biotechnology and in its importance for the school curriculum. This handbook offers teachers:

- an overview of the significance and scope of biotechnology
- an introduction to the content of biotechnology and its relevance to the everyday world
- a guide to how biotechnology fits into the National Curriculum, within and across subject disciplines
- appropriate teaching strategies
- suggestions for practical work
- case studies and other material which can be used directly with sixth form students
- a glossary of terms
- a guide to resources
- coverage of safety issues.

This is an essential resource for practising and trainee teachers of science and technology.

Contents
What is biotechnology? – Biotechnology and the school curriculum – Biotechnology and the food industry – Biotechnology and medicine – Biotechnology in agriculture – Biotechnology and the environment – Biotechnology, fuels and chemicals – Biotechnology through problem solving – Biotechnology through discussion-based learning – Practical considerations – Resources – Glossary – Appendix – References – Index.

176pp   0 335 09368 X (Paperback)   0 335 09369 8 (Hardback)